CATSKILL TRAILS

A Ranger's Guide to the High Peaks

BOOK TWO: THE CENTRAL CATSKILLS

Edward G. Henry

BLACK·DOME

Black Dome Press Corp.
1011 Route 296
Hensonville, New York 12439
Tel: (518) 734-6357
Fax: (518) 734-5802
www.blackdomepress.com

Published by
Black Dome Press Corp.
PO Box 64, Catskill, NY 12414
www.blackdomepress.com

ISBN: 1-883789-23-0

The Library of Congress has catalogued Book One as follows:

Library of Congress Cataloging-in-Publication Data:

Henry, Edward G.

Catskill trails: a ranger's guide to the high peaks/by Edward G. Henry.

p. cm.

Contents: bk. 1. The northern Catskills

ISBN 1-883789-22-2 (trade paper)

1. Hiking--New York (State)--Catskill Mountains--Guidebooks. 2. Trails
--New York (State)--Catskill Mountains--Guidebooks. 3. Catskill
Mountains (N.Y.)--Guidebooks.

GV199.42.N652 C373 2000

00-026162

**Outdoor recreational activities are by their very nature potentially hazardous and
contain risk. Please see CAUTION, pg. 6.**

The maps in this book were created using TOPO! Interactive Maps from Wildflower
Productions. To learn more about digital map products from Wildflower, please visit
www.topo.com or call 415.558.8700

Photos by Edward G. Henry
Catskill Map, copyright © NYS DEC, used by permission.
Design by Carol Clement, Artemisia, Inc.
Printed in the USA

10   9   8   7   6

In memory of
Christopher Andrew Richardson

ACKNOWLEDGMENTS

First of all, I want to thank all my friends who accompanied me on many of my Catskill hikes, especially John Butnor and Shawn Keizer whose companionship on the trail and throughout my life has always been welcomed and enjoyed. Reggie Carlson, Mike Olexa, Billy Kuhne, and a host of others also played a role in joining me on the trails, as reviewers of this book, and as friends and supporters that I always will appreciate, and always have.

The catalyst for this book trails back to Labor Day of 1989 when my friend Sue Ives invited me to go camping in Woodland Valley. Late on that Friday afternoon, she recommended that we hike Wittenberg Mountain. It was a tough hike, but once we crested the peak and the trees parted to reveal the Ashokan Reservoir, eastern Catskills, Hudson Valley, and points east, my eyes and my soul were filled with a new wonder. From that point on, this book was a certainty. Thank you, Sue.

From the professional arena I want to thank all the people who helped bring the book to fruition. Debbie Allen and Steve Hoare at Black Dome Press have been wonderful to work with and very gentle with me. I also want to acknowledge the efforts of John Butnor, Patricia H. Davis, Matina Billias and Doris West Brooks whose experience with words and the Catskills helped polish this work in ways that only their experience and talents could. Carol Clement brought an expertise and efficiency to the production of this book that only a graphic designer who is also a licensed hiking guide could offer. (She and her partners are often found on these very trails guiding for their tour company, High Land Flings Footloose Holidays.)

I thank Dr. Michael Kudish, whose work and occasional correspondence has been of tremendous help to me in learning about the Catskills and its forests. In addition, I want to express how pleased I was to have the editorial and technical help of Jack Sencabaugh on Book One. We may be from a different generation, but we share many of the same loves. Having someone of his caliber associated with my work is, indeed, a pleasure.

I also wish to thank my parents—my Mother for her reviewing and editing skills, and my Father for getting me started with photography, the skill that first got me interested in exploring the Catskill Mountains and the rest of the world.

And to my wife Kerry—I must thank you for putting up with my infatuation with the Catskills and for giving me the time I needed to write this book. Without your love and support an accomplishment such as this could not be so sweet.

CAUTION

Outdoor recreation activities are by their very nature potentially hazardous and contain risk. All participants in such activities must assume the responsibility for their own actions and safety. The outdoors are forever changing. No book can replace good judgment. The author and the publisher cannot be held responsible for inaccuracies, errors or omissions or for changes in the details in this publication or for the consequences of any reliance on the information contained herein or for the safety of people in the outdoors.

HIKING RULES AND GUIDELINES

1. Dress appropriately—cotton clothing and sneakers are the number one cause of illness and injury leading to emergency evacuation.
2. Be prepared—have a first aid kit, whistle, flashlight, matches, small tarp, extra high-energy food, and water.
3. Sign in and out at trail registers.
4. Wear and use appropriate snow gear when the trails are snow-covered.
5. Make sure all campsites are more than 150 feet from a trail or water, or in a designated site.
6. Treat all water before drinking—use chemicals, a filter, or boil for more than two minutes.
7. When camping, hang all food and garbage from a tree at least 50 feet from camp, 15 feet or more above the ground, and 8 feet or more from tree trunks and limbs.
8. Use pre-existing fire rings when possible. Make sure all fires are completely extinguished before breaking camp.
9. Camping permits are needed for groups of 10 or more people, or for one or more people staying in the same place for more than three consecutive nights.
10. Camping and fires are prohibited above 3500 feet between March 22 and December 20 of each year.

And remember: if you carry it in, carry it out!

TABLE OF CONTENTS

Many waterfalls grace Peekamoose Road.

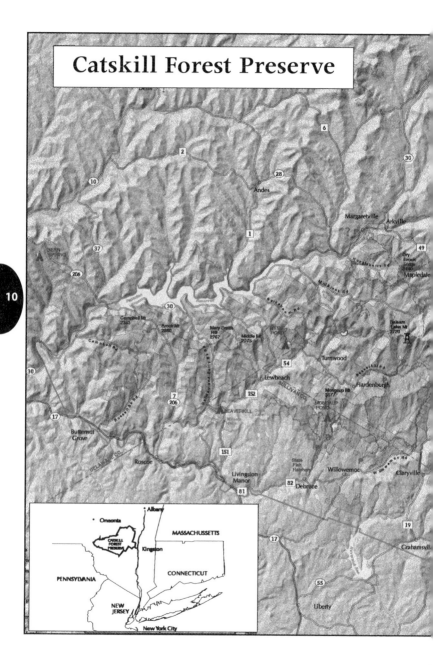

Catskill Forest Preserve

View east from the Balsam Lake Mountain fire tower.

WELCOME TO THE CATSKILLS

To experience the Catskill Mountains through exploration creates a life-long bond. This book uses hiking trails throughout the Catskills as guides to the region's natural history. Each mountain, ridgetop, waterfall, and clove tells its own natural story.

Through photos, personal experiences, and written descriptions, the Catskills' ecology, history, and spirit unfolds. Beautiful mountain vistas, breathtaking waterfalls, and rugged trails become opportunities to discover the forces shaping nature. Silent bedrock cliffs, babbling brooks, and light summer breezes caressing majestic forest stands are part of this experience.

Natural history is an open field. In this book's examination of the Catskills' natural history, it employs forest ecology, geology, meteorology, wildlife biology, geography, economics, and history to reveal a fuller picture of the Catskill Mountains and the interconnected forces that shaped them.

For convenience and continuity, this book divides the Catskills geographically. The southern and western Catskills, a series of low, rounded hills, are not covered. This book concentrates on areas with peaks above 3,500 feet. Delineated by glacial features, the Catskills' high peaks divide into a northern and southern half. This book, the second of a two-volume set, covers the southern half, the central Catskills. In the 1800s, people reinforced this split when they referred to the central Catskills as the Shandaken Mountains. Within each half, closely related peaks make additional groupings; however, many shared characteristics cross these artificial boundaries, the result of arbitrary, human decisions. The mountains are the mountains; they do not divide into neat groups, nor do they heed man's classifications.

Although this work stands alone, it is only a starting place. The Catskills await anyone wishing to explore its slopes. The list of traveled routes is designed to serve as an introduction to further explorations.

PREFACE

I'm pleased you've decided to join me in exploring the Catskills. I'm not sure exactly where we'll go today, for that's up to you, and the Catskills offer many choices. Perhaps we'll visit the Giant Ledge, one of my favorites. As one of the shortest hikes to a mountaintop and a vista in the Catskills, Giant Ledge offers an extraordinary return for the time and effort needed to climb it. The trail, which starts along the Esopus Creek's headwaters, crosses the gathering stream and quickly climbs a mountain spine. A pleasant forest of beech, sugar maple, black cherry, and yellow birch dominate the steep, rocky slopes. Chipmunks dart among the rocks and pileated woodpeckers fill the air with the sound of their probing. Splashes of color—violets, painted trillium, wood sorrel—complement the forest's deciduous green. Golden rays of sunlight stream through the quiltwork leaf canopy to spotlight small patches of forest floor. Although the air is still and warm, the rush of air surging over the mountain ridges fills the background with noise. Large gray sandstone boulders cover much of the ground, more exposed along the trail where people have left their mark on this recovering wilderness; like most of the Catskills these slopes were stripped of their timber to feed the needs of industry. The occasional hemlock, its soft, evergreen needles a shadowy contrast with its deciduous cousins, stands as a living memorial to this consumptive past.

Soon the trail tops the mountain ridge and comes to a four-way intersection. Heading north, the trail becomes flat. The Catskills' horizontal sandstone layers drain poorly, and the thin soils cannot hold much water. As a result, the trail is wet and muddy. Animal tracks such as deer, fox, and even the occasional bear are apparent in the deep mud. The wind now rushes through the stunted trees—mainly yellow birch and black cherry. Here, the growing conditions stunt the trees and limit the species that can survive. The trail conditions improve as it climbs Giant Ledge's last 200 feet of elevation. On first glance, the summit is chaotic, a random assortment of boulders, stunted trees, and sprawling shrubs, but after a few steps the trail leads to a series of open rock ledges and 180-foot cliffs—the mountain's namesake. By far, however, it is the east-facing view that is Giant Ledge's most impressive feature. Woodland Valley lies 1900 feet below, and beyond it rise two of the Catskills' most prominent peaks—Wittenberg and Cornell Mountains. To the south looms the Catskills' highest peak, Slide Mountain. To the north, beyond the jumble of smaller peaks filling the Esopus Valley, the horizon is filled with the Devil's Path Mountains and the rest of the northern Catskills. Perhaps most impressive is the lack of any sign of civilization. While it is not hard to reach, Giant Ledge—a place where one can spend an entire afternoon sunning on a warm rock ledge without noticing time's passage—is worth visiting again and again.

This volume only covers the central Catskills, the area considered "the Shandaken Mountains" in the early and mid-1800s when the mountains to the north and east, including Hunter Mountain and Kaaterskill High Peak, were referred to as the Catskills. While the mountains are all of one origin and history, this artificial, geographic split does makes a distinct break between the Catskills central and northern sections. Starting at the southern wall of Platte Clove and the Devil's Path's southern slopes, this boundary continues to Spruceton Valley's southern wall. Following New York Route 42 south, this division then encounters the Esopus Valley and heads west with it, cresting the Hudson-Delaware divide north of Belleayre Mountain. The mountains south of this line, including Slide Mountain, king of the Catskills, are the subject of this volume (Book Two). The northern Catskills are the subject of Book One.

Most mountainous areas have an elevation status that defines its high peaks. In the Catskills, this number is 3,500 feet. This book includes all the peaks above this "magic" number (with the exception of Graham Mountain, which is on private land with no public access) plus other, lower peaks and areas with significant vistas or other landmarks.

The route to each destination was chosen either because it was the shortest route to the peak or main destination, or because there was something else special along the way that makes taking a longer route worthwhile. Some of the hikes are loops—it is always more fun and interesting to cover new ground than to backtrack, even if it takes a little longer. In some cases, the shortest route entails some very steep slopes, but the challenge and physical rewards of keeping in shape make the tough hikes worthwhile. A few of the routes I use are off-trail and require additional safety awareness. Although some of the routes skirt private land, you should not enter posted land without prior permission; none of the hikes listed here encourage or require trespass. The routes I used to write this book, along with mile notes, are listed in the appendix.

The Catskills are a special place. As I've traveled and explored the Catskill Mountains, I've come to love them and learn from them. The mountains and their stories have become a part of my fabric. Putting this information into a book was almost second nature.

Even though I grew up at the mountains' edge, I did not become attached to the peaks until my sophomore year in college. One weekend, a friend asked me to go camping at Woodland Valley. We hiked to Wittenberg and Giant Ledge. The views were incredible! The rounded mountains, the soft, green forests, the sapphire blue of the Ashokan Reservoir, and the distant horizon in Vermont, Massachusetts, and Connecticut captured my imagination and soul. I was hooked. I started hiking all the peaks and photographing all the views. I used topographic maps to learn the names and shapes of all the mountains. Soon I was putting knowledge I learned in school to work interpreting the Catskills.

And so I experienced the deep roar and cool spray of Kaaterskill Falls, stiff breezes atop Wittenberg Mountain while taking in its incredible vista, and peaceful evenings pondering the pastel pinks, purples, and oranges of a sunset from the Ashokan Reservoir's eastern shore. Each of these scenes is only a small facet of the Catskill Mountain gemstone. I started writing about my experiences, and these efforts led to this book.

While my formal training is in forest ecology and my career is in professional conservation, I use subjects ranging from geology to economics to reveal the Catskill Mountain story. My hope is that you will no longer walk along anonymous trails and see a series of impersonal hills and waterfalls; rather, I hope you will look into the forest and envision past logging and the process of succession, get to know the trees and wildlife, touch the icy waters of a trout stream, smell the honeyed air of spring, taste the tartness of sheep sorrel, and see the remnants and signs of the past ice age. Perhaps you will be able to imagine the Catskills buried in a sea of ice with the exception of Slide Mountain's summit, its peak a lone beacon among the expanse of dirty ice. My hope is that this book can help you experience the mountains in a way more personal and inspirational than just following a series of trail signs ever could be, and that you will experience the Catskills as a natural historian rather than a tourist.

Hiking a mountain peak is a three-dimensional experience, but time, the fourth dimension, is often ignored. With a trained eye, you can see the Catskills not just as they are in the present, but as they looked in the past, and perhaps how they will appear in the future. The story of the Catskills is more than 500 million years old, but as easy to read as picking up a rock or looking at a rounded mountaintop. By exploring the Catskills through time, you will experience the rise and fall of great mountain ranges, ice ages, changing forests, and man's economic activity.

There are a few things I cannot stress enough when you are exploring the Catskills. First, wear appropriate footwear. If your feet are not happy, you will not be happy, no matter how great the view. Second, always have enough water for your trip. Whether you carry it in, use a filter, or chemically treat your water, make sure you have enough. Do not drink untreated water, as it can have *giardia*, a disease that will turn your digestive system inside-out for months. Third, bring a map and compass along with you. It's always good to have an idea of where you are in the mountains, and it will help you maintain a sense of direction. The best hiking maps to Catskill Mountain trails are produced by the New York-New Jersey Trail Conference, which also coordinates volunteer trail maintenance efforts in the region (www.nynjtc.org). As global positioning satellite units (often referred to as GPS units) become more affordable and reliable, they will become another option for remaining oriented in the forest. Used properly, a GPS makes it almost impossible to get lost. Some would even call using a GPS "cheating." In addition, carrying a small first aid kit and dressing for the weather are two other essential safety tips.

The Catskill Mountains are part of an ongoing process. Mother Nature never finishes her landscapes, but she works on a time scale much longer than a human lifespan. We may never see the mountains as any different than they look today, but we do play a role in their current appearance. Perhaps the most disturbing thing visitors do is litter. Whether it's a soda can a quarter-mile from the trailhead, or a 40-year-old candy wrapper along the top ridge of a trail-less mountain peak, it sends the message, "I don't care." While most people do not litter, neither do most of us pick up litter left by others. If there is one favor I would ask as you explore the Catskills, it is to please try and leave the place a little cleaner than you found it. If we all did that, man's garbage would not escort us to most of the mountaintops, and all those little pieces of litter would not slap the concept of wilderness in the face.

The Catskills' story is a long and complex tale, but it is not too hard to follow if you know what to look for in the landscape. I have attempted to bring to you as much of this story as possible, and give you the ability to look deeper for yourselves. And maybe, if I've done a good job, I'll be able to transplant to you a little bit of my love for the Catskills.

An Introduction to the Catskills

The Catskill Mountains rise west of the Hudson River in south-eastern New York, roughly 100 miles north-northwest of New York City. The highest peaks are in Ulster and Greene Counties. Lower mountains associated with the Catskills stretch into Delaware, Sullivan, and Schoharie Counties. Elevations of the Catskills' 50 highest summits range from 3,400 to 4,180 feet. The highest peaks, those above 3,500 feet, form the Catskill High Peaks, and are the basis for the Catskill 3500 Club; club membership requires hiking all of these peaks.

In the eastern Catskills, a spruce-fir forest dominates elevations above 3,300 feet. Most western summits support balsam fir forests or upper hardwoods. Northern hardwoods, mainly sugar maple, beech, and yellow birch, cover the middle and lower slopes. Hemlock forests line most stream courses. The lowland valleys often contain mixed hardwood species, while pine-oak forests grace the dry, exposed ridges.

Trout lilies.

The Catskills have a cool, moist climate characterized by mild summers and cold winters. Mean average temperature at 3,000 feet is 38F degrees: 61F degrees in July, and 14F degrees in January. The growing season lasts about 120 days. The high summits in the moister eastern Catskills receive about 65 inches of annual precipitation. Drier western summits get about 50 inches. Slide Mountain, the wettest peak, receives 70 inches each year. Snow accounts for 20 percent of annual precipitation, an average of 140 inches.

Set 100 miles north and west of the Atlantic Ocean, the ocean does not influence local temperature; however, as ocean moisture moves inland and rises, orographic (mountain influenced) precipitation arises. Precipitation in the eastern and southern Catskills is up to a third greater than surrounding valleys. Orographic lifting also influences temperature, producing a 3-5°F change for each 1,000 feet. The city of Kingston, at sea level on the Hudson River, averages 16F degrees warmer than Slide Mountain's summit.

Wind is another major factor in the Catskills' upper elevations. Mountain and valley breezes develop on most sunny days. Prevailing winds are from the west. The mountains enhance winds associated with fronts and storms. Gusts of 40 miles per hour and higher are common.

The first white men to see the Catskills were the crew on Henry Hudson's ship, *Half Moon*, in September of 1609. At that time, Indian tribes living between the river and the Catskill Mountains were mainly of the Minnisink and Delaware tribes. To the north were the Mohawks, fearsome warriors of the Iroquois Confederacy. Indians generally avoided the Catskills, preferring the warmer climates of the surrounding valleys, but summer hunting parties frequented the mountains.

Early European settlement was Dutch, an influence remaining through place names and spellings. Many streams retain the Dutch suffix of "kill." The name Catskill may derive from the Dutch for "wildcat stream." Bobcats, and some people claim mountain lions as well, still roam the mountains. The Catskills were also called the Blue or Blew Mountains, due to their color and harsh weather.

A youthful Catskill Mountain stream.

The fertile, mild climate of the Hudson Valley attracted many settlers. Huge estates and small farmsteads lined both riverbanks. While many had beautiful views of the Catskills, few settlers did more than ponder that beauty from the civilized valleys.

Conflicts in the mid-1660s led to English occupation and rule, but life changed little for the Dutch settlers, and few troubles arose. Like the Dutch, the English discouraged westward expansion, yet even without governmental policy Europeans shunned the Catskills, associating the foreboding mountains with evil spirits. Settlers spread into the valleys slowly, but it was not until logging concerns invaded the Catskills that society lost this irrational fear.

Among the strongest events discouraging settlement was a famous land deal, the Hardenburgh Patent. A grant of 2 million acres to Johannis Hardenburgh in 1708 kept the Catskills closed to settlement, and opened legal battles lasting into the 20th century. The grant included most of what is now Ulster, Greene, Sullivan, and Delaware Counties. Eventually, the Livingstons and other prominent families bought into the land grant.

Oaks are common along the eastern escarpment.

As more and more people came to the Hudson Valley, some settlers began to move into the mountains to make a new life and find greater freedom. But farming the Catskills was difficult. The land, covered with only a thin soil, did not retain fertility. Bound to the land through long-term contracts, local residents lived a difficult and poor life. Few people had the freedom to leave or to explore the mountains.

Along with agriculture, forestry became a major industry. Throughout the mid-1800s, tanneries cut the Catskills' mighty hemlock stands for their bark, a source of tannin, which was used in leather production. Raw hides came to the Catskills from as far away as Argentina. Within a few decades, the Catskill forests lay in ruin. Without the hemlocks, the tanning industry collapsed and the region's prosperity ended. Until the mid-1900s, the Catskills would be socioeconomically considered part of Appalachia.

The Catskills' only recognized natural resources were building stone and trees. Stripped of their timber, economic ruin characterized the Catskill Mountains in the late 1800s. Only tourism remained viable, and it declined beginning in the early 1900s. Time and opportunity drew people away and, eventually, the sparsely settled region provided a better livelihood for those remaining. In 1885, New York State formed the Catskill State Park from the abandoned and abused mountains, and as New York City grew, the Catskills' clean water became a major natural resource, a fact not lost to politicians and businessmen when considering the Park's creation.

Today, the Catskill State Park encompasses more than 700,000 acres, a third directly stewarded by New York State. Much of the land is set aside by the New York State Constitution as "forever wild." Most of the high peaks lie within the publicly owned Park. The preserved and recovering lands provide sanctuary, wilderness, and adventure for visitors and residents. Despite debates over the role of government in land ownership and use, the rejuvenated Catskills are a natural resource whose current ecological value is beyond question. To explore the Catskills is to experience the beauty, diversity, and abundance thriving in the mountains.

Typical Catskill Mountain sandstone.

A BRIEF GEOLOGIC HISTORY
OF THE CATSKILL MOUNTAINS

The Catskills are one-sided mountains. Many appear cast from the same mold—a steep eastern front builds to a summit, followed by a gentle western slope. Northern slopes have fewer side ridges than southern faces. Despite the passage of 380 million years since their formation, the Catskills' strata display similar physical characteristics that evolved under shared environmental conditions.

On a smaller scale, individual mountains display distinctive characteristics as ice, water, and wind eroded each peak differently. Mountains appearing identical from one side reveal distinctive subtleties from other perspectives. A rounded slope out of place, a shoulder dipping at a different angle, a deeper notch, or a steeper summit— each individualizes the mountains.

Geographically part of the Appalachians, the Catskills are the highest section of the Allegheny Plateau. The uplifted plateau evolved into mountains as erosion dissected the high, level surface. Running west of the Appalachians and parallel to them, this eroded plateau runs from New York to Tennessee. Other well-known regions of the Allegheny Plateau include Pennsylvania's Pocono Mountains and the Cumberland Plateau in Kentucky and Tennessee.

The Appalachian Mountains parallel North America's east coast, constantly struggling against erosion. Stretching from Maine to Alabama within the United States, these quiet, picturesque mountains reveal few clues to their rugged past. The highest point remaining in the North American Appalachians is North Carolina's Mount Mitchell at 6,684 feet above sea level.

The Appalachians, however, extend far beyond the United States. They cross into Canada as the Shuckstacks before they slide into the Atlantic Ocean. When the ocean formed, its waters split the great mountain chain. The range emerges from the Atlantic as Scotland's Caledonian Mountains. They rise again from the Baltic Sea as Norway's fjords and mountains. The chain's highest peak is Norway's Mount Goldhopiggen at 8,097 feet above sea level.

The Catskills' geologic history began long before the formation of its rocks. Events of the past 1.1 billion years created complex geologic structures below the area's present surface strata. Entire mountain chains rose and eroded on the land currently topped by the Catskills. Seas lapped against sandy beaches and great fern forests thrived on coastal plains.

The Catskills' exposed Devonian sandstones and shales sit atop these rocks. Their perseverance, or lack of it, influenced the Catskills' geologic evolution. North America is more than one billion years old. As geologic eras passed, North America grew, condensed, and changed. As it drifted, its orientation also changed. While continental positions in this book are relative to their current locations, keep in mind that North America wandered during the past billion years. At the time of the Appalachian Orogeny (mountain building event), 290 million years ago, North America's east coast sat along the equator.

North America's Precambrian history is poorly understood. The rock record reveals more questions than it answers. Beyond the creation of the region's basement rock, few events this old relate to the Catskills. The Taconic Orogeny, which occurred 450 million years ago, is the first well-defined geological event affecting the Catskills.

The Taconic Mountains lifted as North America and Northern Europe (called Baltica) collided. Together, these land masses formed the Old Red Sandstone Continent. Few features remain from these ancient mountains. Rivers, with the help of wind and ice, eroded the range particle by particle, filling a basin to the west. Although the mountains no longer exist, the river systems that carried them away are seen in the rocks of the Queenston Delta. Buried beneath the Catskills, these rocks surface from western New York to Ohio. Today, the Taconic Mountains' stumps are the Taconic Hills in eastern New York and the Berkshires in western New England. From many Catskill summits, these hills define the eastern horizon.

Once the Earth's forces settled, the Taconics stopped lifting and began to erode. At this time, Gondwana, which included southern

Europe, Florida, Africa, and South America, pushed toward the Old Red Sandstone Continent. An ocean, the Iapetus, separated the two land masses. Britain and a volcanic island chain, Avalon, split the Iapetus Ocean into eastern and western halves.

With the Taconics eroding, an inland sea invaded eastern North America. Corals thrived in these shallow tropical waters. Thick, calcium-rich layers covered the Queenston Delta while it began its transition to rock. The corals that lived during the Ordovician period formed limestone, and some evolved into dolomite. These calcareous rocks lie beneath the Catskills' sandstones and shales. They surface north and east of the Catskills in the Hudson, Mohawk, Schoharie, Esopus, and Wallkill Valleys. In some places, a few thin layers of limestone mix with the Catskills' lower strata. Plant species requiring high calcium levels thrive near these layers.

The sediments forming the Catskills' strata originated from an extinct mountain chain. The Acadian Mountains, born in the Silurian Era 380 million years ago, formed as Avalon and North America collided. Set along North America's east coast, the Acadian Mountains rose 25,000 feet above sea level. Their peaks danced with the clouds. During this same time period, the British Isles melded with Baltica (part of the Old Red Sandstone Continent at the time), an event that closed the eastern Iapetus Ocean.

Millions of years passed. During the Devonian Period the western Iapetus contracted as Gondwana (formed of a merged southern Europe, South America, and Africa) moved toward North America and Baltica. As the Acadian Mountains eroded, sediments that would become the Catskills migrated west into a shallow inland sea. As its basin filled, its shores retreated westward. A progression of size-sorted sediments formed, the clays and silts traveling farther than the sands. The sands often dropped from the rivers as they entered their deltas. Cross-bedding patterns preserved in the Catskills' sandstones reflect this deposition. As the inland sea evaporated and retreated, it left a salt layer. This layer sits beneath the Catskills' strata. Since salts flow under high pressure, they form weak rock, shifting and cracking rocks above them. At the surface, these movements result in jointing—a major feature found within the Catskills' sandstones.

A series of rivers transported the eroding Acadian Mountains to the sea. Sediment loads accumulated as waters slowed in lowland areas. Together, these sediments form the Catskill Clastic Wedge, better known as the Catskill Delta. The landscape resembled America's Gulf Coast. After 50 million years, the Acadian Mountains evolved into a peneplain (flat surface). Sedimentary rocks derived from these mountains stretch from the Catskills' eastern escarpment to the Pennsylvania-Ohio border. Sediments from the Acadian Mountains accumulated as 15,000 feet of sand, silt, and clay. Thickest near the mountains' base, these sediments covered the future Hudson Valley (there was no Hudson River until 75 million years ago) and the Taconics' stumps.

The Devonian and Mississippian Periods passed, and the Iapetus Ocean began to close. Gondwana and the Old Red Sandstone Continent drifted together. Friction built, and volcanoes erupted in the shrinking ocean to form an archipelago off North America's east coast. The island chain resembled Japan. All the while, North America and Africa continued on a collision course, dooming the young islands trapped between them. The Iapetus Ocean perished when North America and Africa collided. This event also bonded northern and southern Europe and cemented Florida to North America. The resulting uplift would become the Appalachian Mountains.

When the Appalachian Orogeny began 290 million years ago, it marked the birth of the super-continent Pangea. During this time, the Appalachians were the world's greatest mountain range, spanning eastern North America and northern Europe. Ever since, some remnant of these mountains has remained along North America's east coast.

During this mountain-building event, hundreds of miles of rock in eastern North America bent, folded, and faulted. In contrast with these deformed rocks, including the neighboring Shawangunks, the Catskill Delta did not buckle. Removed from the collision, the delta rose 7,500 feet, but no horizontal deformation occurred. The Acadian Mountains' sediments, now hardened into rock, became the template for the Catskill Plateau.

In time, the Earth's forces split Pangea, and a new ocean formed. Europe and Africa retreated from North America and created the Atlantic Ocean. Centered on the Mid-Atlantic Ridge, this ocean continues to expand as it pushes adjoining continental plates.

The Earth heaved and buckled when the Appalachians formed, yet erosion's ever-present forces immediately began removing the land. Water, wind, and ice weathered the rock, forming steep slopes, sharp ravines and deep valleys. The sediment-laden waters gathered into nameless rivers, most long extinct, and descended toward the precursors of the Atlantic Ocean and Gulf of Mexico.

Differential erosion sculpted the Catskill plateau into mountains. Unlike most mountains that form from faulted and folded rocks, the Catskills eroded from a plateau into peaks, valleys, and gorges. More than 7,500 feet of sediments compose the Catskills. Half lie below sea level, and sediment depth decreases to the west. Most sediments eroded from the Catskills flow into the Hudson River; all enter the Atlantic Ocean. Ice ages rounded the peaks and widened the valleys. Steep cloves and tumbling waterfalls result.

The Catskills abruptly end at their eastern escarpment. No trace of the Catskill Delta remains east of this point. The Hudson Valley occupies the gap, but geologists do not know if the Hudson River, which is only 75 million years old, was around to remove the sediments. The Catskills' disappearing sediments remain a geologic mystery.

The highest point remaining on this ancient plateau is 4,180-foot Slide Mountain. Most of the Catskill summits reach 3,400-3,800 feet. Areas with weaker rocks eroded faster, becoming the valleys. The erosion continues, and streams constantly transport sediments released by physical and chemical weathering. Rock slides move material downslope, scarring the landscape. In the early 1820s, a massive 1,200-foot landslide reworked Slide Mountain's northeastern face, naming the mountain in the process. Other large slides affected Wittenberg, Blackhead, Sugarloaf, and Friday Mountains.

A hard, erosion-resistant conglomerate called Catskill Puddingstone caps many of the Catskills' highest summits. As the current mountaintop bedrock, it shows signs of heavy erosion. Studded with rounded quartz pebbles from the Acadian Mountains, it erodes into a pebble-filled gravel. Other peaks have a hard, coarse-grained sandstone. Beneath these caprocks are the Hamilton and Oneonta formations. Kaaterskill Falls reveals the junction between these two rock types. Throughout the Catskills, resistant Hamilton sandstones support ridges, while shales erode into deep valleys.

Besides stream, water, and wind erosion, glaciation played a role in shaping the Catskills. Although many ice sheets buried and altered the region, only the most recent advances show signs of passage. The Wisconsin Ice Sheet moved south 100,000 years ago, obliterating past signs of glaciation. This continental ice sheet culminated 22,000 years ago during a surge known as the Woodfordian advance. Barely covering the Catskills, this advance may not have buried Slide Mountain's summit. Slide's isolated peak, a nanatak, would have protruded as a lonely rock beacon among a sea of ice.

As the Wisconsin Ice Sheet spread into New York, it faced two major barriers: the Adirondack and Catskill Mountains. The two ranges funneled the ice into adjoining lowlands. Ice plowed through the Champlain, Hudson, and Mohawk Valleys. It moved into the Catskills slowly. The mountains diverted the main ice tongue into the Mid-Hudson Valley. A smaller tongue penetrated the mountains via the Schoharie Valley. Moving south and east through the Schoharie and its tributaries, it reached the escarpment wall's backside. The 3,000-foot wall prevented the ice from merging with the Hudson Valley lobe.

Ice from the Hudson Valley scoured Kaaterskill and Platte Cloves. Eventually, it spilled over the cloves' walls, joining ice from the Schoharie Valley. Heavily eroded by ice, the northern Catskills reflect their glaciated past. While the ice built in the cloves, small ice tongues pushed though the Devil's Path notches: Jimmy Dolan Notch, Pecoy Notch, Mink Hollow, and Stony Clove.

The southeastern Catskills remained free of ice for longer periods. After the Woodfordian surge, lesser glacial episodes invaded the northern and eastern Catskills. The Wagon Wheel advance, occurring 17,000 years ago, penetrated well into the Esopus Valley to lap against the central high peaks. A final glacial onslaught, the Grand Gorge advance, developed 16,000 years ago. Ice tongues poured into the Schoharie Valley and topped the escarpment wall at Kaaterskill and Platte Cloves, further carving and eroding the northeastern Catskills. Alpine glaciation redeveloped in the southern and western Catskills enhancing the area's more complex local topography.

As Earth's climate warmed, the ice sheets melted faster than they advanced. Ice melted from the southern Catskills first. As the Wisconsin Ice Sheet disintegrated, ice dams hemmed large glacial lakes. Except for the rock flours and delta terraces that coated lake bottoms, few signs of these short-lived lakes remain. Large meltwater rivers widened valleys while cutting and enlarging gaps. Underfit valleys and steep, rounded notches resulted. Underfit valleys form when torrents of glacial meltwater widen valleys far beyond their original size. After the ice melts and no longer provides the large volumes of water, the remaining river valley is much wider than needed to hold the river. Underfit valleys in the Catskills include the Delaware and Susquehanna Rivers, and the Esopus and Schoharie Creeks. Prominent notches include Stony Clove and Mill Wheel Gap.

When the glaciers retreated, they left behind the material carried within the ice. Glacial tills—unsorted sediments carried in the ice—cover the entire region. Deepest in the valleys, the tills thin toward mountain summits. Transported boulders, most local, but some from as far away as the Adirondacks and Canada, pepper the landscape.

Current temperature measurements estimate the northern Catskills to be .5F degrees cooler than the southern Catskills. Combined with topography, this temperature difference would help account for the continental ice sheet's longer presence in the northern Catskills. After the Wisconsin Ice Sheet retreated, and during the Grand Gorge advance, the region remained cold enough to maintain alpine glaciers. The deeply carved hollows and spur ridges distinctive to the southern Catskills reflect this alpine glaciation. Smoother, more rounded slopes characterize the northern Catskills. Rock formations and stream erosion perpetuated these differences.

Alpine glaciers scalloped many of the southern peaks. Cirques are the most common alpine feature. As ice flowed down the mountainside, it eroded the land beneath it. A cirque-scalloped mountain often resembles two arms wrapped around a body. Good examples of these formations sculpt Mt. Tremper, Overlook Mountain, Ashokan High Point, and Balsam Mountain. Echo Lake, between Overlook and Plattekill Mountains, is the Catskills' most developed cirque. Panther Mountain, home to the Catskills' last alpine glacier, is the mountains' largest.

As the warming trend continued, the last remnants of the Grand Gorge advance melted. Unlike the southern Catskills' south-flowing rivers, the northern Catskills drain into the north-flowing Schoharie Creek. Dammed by retreating ice, the Schoharie Valley became a glacial lake. Vroman's Nose, west of Middleburgh, New York, provides a great overview of this ancient lake bed. The region's fertile farmlands result from the sediments deposited in this short-lived lake. The quickly warming climate limited alpine glacier formation in the northern Catskills, and the ice sheet continued its steady northward retreat.

Other signs of glaciation also mark the Catskills. North and South Lakes, located along the eastern escarpment, are kettle lakes. They formed when trapped ice blocks melted in poorly drained ground. Rainwater and a man-made dam enhance and replenish these lakes. Glacial striations recorded ice sheet movement as hard rocks in the ice scratched softer bedrock. Strong striations mark many Catskill Mountains, including Overlook, North, and Peekamoose.

Among the Catskills' largest glacial features was a huge ice dam that stretched between Overlook Mountain and Ashokan High Point during the Wagon Wheel advance. The resulting lake submerged the entire Esopus Valley. The lake cut Mill Wheel Gap on Ashokan High Point's southeastern flank as it drained.

The formation of the Catskills' cloves and their relation to the Ice Age is well-established. Ice sheets, probably related to the Illinoisian advance one million years ago, first gouged the Catskills' cloves. Subsequent glacial advances scoured and steepened already rugged slopes. In the present time, these cloves hold steep watercourses that continue to carve into their mountain walls. Caught between the surrounding mountain peaks, these streambeds drop more than 1,000 feet per mile.

The Catskills have three major cloves: Kaaterskill Clove, Platte Clove, and Woodland Valley. Often inaccessible, people rarely visit the isolated streambeds. Platte Clove is the Catskills' most rugged area. Within its reaches are 14 waterfalls higher than 20 feet. Best known for their scenery and waterfalls, the cloves attract many summer visitors to their more accessible flanks. Kaaterskill Clove is home to Kaaterskill Falls, New York's highest waterfall. Woodland Valley's steep slopes nestle against Slide Mountain.

Water continues to erode the Catskills.

Catskill soils directly relate to the area's past glacial activity. Most are inceptisols (young, poorly developed soils) derived from materials left by the last ice sheet, recent erosion, and biological processes. Slide Mountain's summit, which probably remained uncovered during the last continental ice sheet, has an older soil. The Catskills' mineral soil evolved from glacial till and outwash. In valleys, these tills can reach 200 feet deep, but mountaintops often have only an inch or two. Rocks are endemic in local soils as attested on the region's farms. Thousands of miles of stone fences run throughout the Catskills. Fragipans—soils bonded into a natural cement—occur frequently. Plant roots cannot penetrate fragipans, restricting growth and support.

The Catskills' rocks are an encrypted guidebook to the mountains' geology. Earthquakes, ancient seas, and possibly, meteorite impacts helped shape the Catskills. Traces of this past remain bound in local rocks. The Acadian Mountains were a constant sediment source throughout the Devonian Period. Along with plant and animal remains, they created a continuous fossil and deposition record. Although few large fossils have been found, an excellent fossil record developed. The Catskills preserve the most complete record of Earth's Devonian history. Local rocks link events throughout the prehistoric world, serving as a template for other dating studies. The area's steady deposition of eroded material is free of faulting, folding, or bending. It is an easy record to read and understand.

Catskill fossil explorations often end in disappointment. Few good specimens are large enough to be considered noteworthy; however, near Gilboa Dam is a petrified forest. The fern-like trees grew 40 feet high. During the age of fishes, these unpopulated forests resembled modern palm forests. The western Catskills contain scattered fossil beds of marine and freshwater fish. Brachiopods, clam-like mollusks, are also common. The Catskills' only economically valuable non-living resources are water and bluestone. Early explorers told wild stories of gold and silver, but none proved true. Along the range's southeastern edge an unusual deposit of selenite gypsum crystals formed from the retreating freshwater sea. Some people believe that oil lies beneath the mountains and that regional water interests suppress this information. While oil shales are common, and a potential source for future oil, no geological evidence supports claims of oil beneath the Catskills.

The Panther Mountain Circle is a puzzling and unique Catskill landform. Together, the Esopus Creek and Woodland Valley outline an almost four-mile circle. Panther Mountain's summit dominates the circle's center. Topographic studies and satellite photos raise further questions about this conspicuous feature. One hypothesis suggests that this circle outlines a meteorite crater. The region lay beneath a shallow sea when the impact occurred. Salt domes, like those found along the Mississippi Delta, are another possibility. A third hypothesis combines these ideas, proposing that after impact, the sea bed broke, crumbled, and distorted, forming a deep pool. When the sea retreated, the isolated pool evaporated and left the salt deposits.

Although a crater would form on impact, the current landscape rises into a 3,720-foot mountain. This apparent paradox could occur because salt and crushed rock are less dense than intact rock. Large amounts of lighter materials will produce a gravitational low point. With less gravity, erosional potentials are decreased. A natural, radial drainage pattern accented the process. Millions of years magnified the gravitational low point, producing an uplifted area. Panther Mountain's rugged terrain makes accurate measurements difficult. Research continues into this mystery.

THE ESOPUS VALLEY

The mountains surrounding the Esopus Valley faced the direct onslaught of the Wisconsin Ice Sheet. Although they still retain more character than mountains to the north, they lost much elevation to the intruding ice. The Esopus Valley's depth provides these peaks their current elevational spread and exaggerated stature. Since these mountains are located near settlements and fertile valleys, people were able to easily strip the area of its resources. Man's impact remains readily apparent throughout this area. Tremper Mountain was among the most exploited. The Ashokan Reservoir holds water for New York City and provides a spectacular setting for the nearby mountains. Ashokan High Point reveals the area's most spectacular view.

A thunderstorm forms above the reservoir's lower basin.

SCENIC RESERVOIR: THE ASHOKAN
AND SURROUNDING LANDS

The Ashokan Reservoir Driving Tour:
Mile: 0.0: Begin at eastern terminus of Basin Road
    1.1: Turn right onto Route 28A
    9.6: Right on Reservoir Road which ends at NY 28 (14.0)

Throughout its history, New York City's economy has been dependent on its connections with the Catskill Mountains. Colonial New Amsterdam, the Dutch name for this port city, received furs, lumber, and agricultural products from the northern settlements. In return, manufactured goods moved upriver. Over time the connection changed—the Catskills became a retreat from the city and a recovering wilderness. Despite changes in the relationship, the link remains strong.

With the tremendous growth of the New World's richest city, its needs quickly surpassed its resource base. Nowhere is this dependence more apparent than with drinking water. By the late 1800s, local water sources became polluted or exploited beyond capacity, and the city tapped upstate watersheds—first the Croton River, then the Catskills.

Soon, the Catskills supplied most of New York City's water—89% by the late 1960s. Although threatened by natural and man-made fertilizer inputs, the Catskills continue to provide some of the world's cleanest water, thanks to the mountains' porous sandstones and shales.

The Ashokan Reservoir, nestled near the Catskills' highest peaks, is the system's cornerstone. More than a 132 billion-gallon storage tank, the reservoir provides other qualities to the local environment. Twelve square miles of open water unveil the neighboring Catskills with views unknown to past generations. The Ashokan, completed in 1919, at a cost $12 million, was the first of New York's Catskill reservoirs. It remains the largest. Considered a man-made wonder of the world, it was one of the largest projects ever undertaken. The blood, sweat, and tears of more than 3,000 workers created the hand-built reservoir. People moved entire towns or watched them die, along with railroads, roads, and streams.

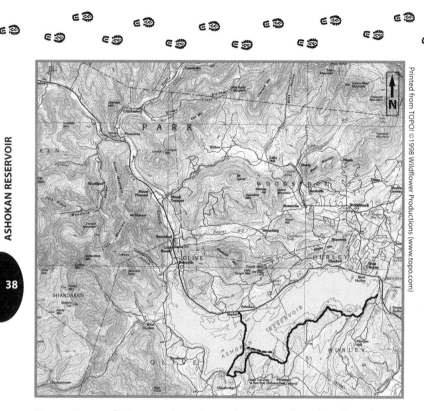

For sanitary, religious, and sentimental reasons, the relocation of more than 2,000 graves accompanied the living residents.

The Ashokan's construction, begun in 1912, ignited controversies that still smoulder. Does New York City have the right to manage lands outside its jurisdiction? Lawyers and politicians from city, state, and local interests continuously argue about land and water rights. Most of the time they accomplish little, frustrate locals, and annoy city water boards.

While the legal and political waters are choppy, the reservoir's are calm, clear, and peaceful. Spread throughout the Catskills, New York City's reservoirs include the Ashokan, Pepacton, Cannonsville, Neversink, Rondout, and Schoharie. Together they impound the world's best municipal water supply. The Ashokan, however, reveals the best scenery.

More than 50 miles of roads encircle the reservoir. They make picturesque, enjoyable drives throughout the year. Beautiful scenery invites frequent stops. Complementing the roads are pleasant walkways that provide charming vistas. A summer evening walk along the quiet waters reveals sunsets rivaling any on the planet. The reservoir's visual impact is spectacular, but a deeper understanding of local natural history enhances the pictures. A story of land and water, it adds awe, value, and comfort to the Ashokan's setting.

A good place to start touring the reservoir is along Basin Road. It skirts the Ashokan's southeastern edge. After a short journey through a pine-oak forest, the reservoir's sparkling waters spread north and west toward distant mountain summits. Basin Road overlooks the reservoir's lower half, revealing a wide Catskill Mountain panorama. When full, the lower basin's water level rests 587 feet above sea level. In winter, this area often receives reservoir-effect snow as storms collect extra moisture when crossing the water.

Split into two groups, some of the Catskills' highest peaks line the Ashokan. One group looms as the northern skyline, while the other rests on the western horizon. The northern mountains lead the eye to 3,150-foot Overlook Mountain. Its slopes anchor the Catskills' eastern escarpment. Local Indians called the 2,000-foot escarpment the Great Wall of Manitou. They believed their spirit-gods lived behind its steep slopes.

Overlook Mountain's backbone boasts a 300-foot television tower. A bright flashing light announces the tower to pilots. This beacon also advertises the visual price of development. Near the tower's base are the Overlook Mountain House's unfinished ruins. Behind Overlook, Plattekill Mountain's eastern slopes merge into the Hudson Valley. Guardian Mountain is west of Overlook. The low slopes of Ohayo Mountain fill the foreground. Until the early 1900s, this 1,300-foot peak held the name Ohio Mountain.

A higher ridge, the Devil's Path, stands beyond these peaks. Overlook eclipses most of Indian Head Mountain, then the Devil's Path continues westward, climbing Twin and Sugarloaf Mountains. Sugarloaf melts into Mink Hollow, an area settled by the survivors of Shays' Rebellion. The rebellion, led by American Revolutionary War

Captain Daniel Shays, occurred in Massachusetts. Rebels wanted a sound national currency and opposed laws discriminatory to farmers and the working poor. More than 1,200 rebels attacked the Springfield, Massachusetts armory on January 25, 1787. They were routed by state militia, and many of the insurgents left Massachusetts for the Catskills to begin new lives.

Plateau Mountain's 3,840-foot summit, the highest point among the nearby northern peaks, lifts from Mink Hollow. Olderbark Mountain spreads southwest from Plateau's main ridge.

Tycetonyk Mountain's triangular outline holds the northwestern foreground. Its 2,500-foot mass separates the northern and western mountains. Tycetonyk marks the summer sunset, when delicate pinks, purples, reds, and blues frame its summit. In autumn, these colors shift south to gather above the Burroughs Range that include some of Catskills' highest peaks. Their name pays tribute to John Burroughs, the famous 19th-century naturalist. The Burroughs Range culminates as 4,180-foot Slide Mountain, the Catskills' highest point and one of Burroughs' favorite camping spots.

South of the Burroughs Range, 3,847-foot Table Mountain and 3,843-foot Peekamoose Mountain complete the western skyline. Ashokan High Point frames the reservoir's southern shore. Wagon Wheel Gap makes a large gash on that 3,098-foot mountain's eastern side. The gap formed when a glacial lake broke through and quickly eroded the mountain wall. A large, almost abandoned stream bed, complete with dry waterfalls, accompany this cut in the mountain.

More than any other mountain, Ashokan High Point embodies the reservoir's beauty. The three-tiered mountain is one of the Catskills' most picturesque peaks, attracting painters, photographers, and naturalists for the past two centuries. Excellent views of the reservoir open from its upper slopes.

Basin Road heads southwest for a mile before spilling onto New York Route 28A. Route 28 speeds along the reservoir's northern shore, while its offspring, Route 28A, winds along its southern edge. Both roads reveal only limited glances at the water, but 28A gives a more thorough tour. Maples, beech, pines, oaks, and hemlock, growing since the early 1920s, block the reservoir from view. Momentary glimpses show the area's varied terrain.

Wildlife thrives in and around the reservoir. Trout, walleye, and bass are common game fish. Protected from hunting, deer, bears, fox, bobcats and a host of small mammals live near the water. A few bald eagles nest along some of the isolated coves. Owls, songbirds, turkey, and grouse also live in the protected basin.

Along the upper basin's southeastern edge, Reservoir Road tops the 191-foot earthen dam restraining Esopus Creek. The site was once a major local landmark known as Bishop's Falls. From the road, a look northeast reveals Tycetonyk and Tonche Mountains. To the west, the peaks slowly shift position as the road parallels their main axis. Then, the road plunges into the forest again.

A small turnoff, Monument Road, heads east from Reservoir Road and winds through a pine-oak forest. Lined by majestic rows of red pine, the needle carpeted pathway leads to a tall stone monument, the Waldo Smith Memorial. Smith was the project engineer during the Ashokan's construction.

Winter at the dividing weir.

Planted red pines surround the monument and most of the reservoir. Red pine is a preferred species around water supplies as it grows quickly, and its roots act as a natural filtration system, reducing fungal and bacterial growth rates and sterilizing soils. Red pine needles decompose slowly, preventing large nutrient inputs from fostering algae growth. Unfortunately, red pine fall victim to many diseases; dead trees are common. Also, in order to germinate, their serotinous cones require intense heat. With fire suppression as a standard land management practice, red pine seeds rarely sprout.

Reservoir Road splits the Ashokan in two, following the retaining wall separating the basins. It passes two stone and concrete pumphouses and continues north to Route 28. Along this narrow road, views open in all directions, history unfolds, and opportunities to enjoy the Ashokan on foot begin. After miles of close forest, the wide-ranging vistas are a complete change of perspective.

The spillway marks the reservoir's heart and provides the area's most spectacular scenery. The spillway reveals the three-foot difference in water level between the basins. When full, the upper water level of the upper basin rests at 590 feet above sea level, but levels often vary with seasonal precipitation patterns.

The area surrounding the pumphouses opens into a 270-degree panorama. The views spread in every direction except southeast. Mountains climb from the reservoir's shoreline to touch the sky. Ashokan High Point holds the reservoir's southern flank, and the Burroughs Range fills the western theater.

The two mountains in the northeast appear to share stature and symmetry. Overlook Mountain is the duo's southern member. Indian Head Mountain is to the north. The mountain's profile explains its name. They appear similar in elevation, but it is a trick of distance. Indian Head reaches a lofty 3,573 feet, while Overlook tops off at 3,150 feet.

West of these two peaks are Tycetonyk and Tonche Mountains. Farther west, the central Catskills unfold about the Esopus Valley. This Catskill symphony begins with Mount Tremper and Mount Pleasant. Both play only a supporting role, neither reaching 3,000 feet. Panther Mountain's northern flank crescendos to 3,720 feet, but remains only a background harmony.

Cross Mountain connects Mount Pleasant with Wittenberg Mountain, first of the Burroughs Range. In front of this range, Samuels Point trails from Wittenberg's 3,780-foot summit. From Wittenberg's peak, an outstanding view of the Ashokan Reservoir unfolds.

The melody continues with Cornell Mountain rising south of Wittenberg. Cornell's 3,860-foot peak is the highest point bounding the Ashokan Reservoir. The ridge falls and lifts again as Friday Mountain. Friday's untrailed slopes hold the Catskills' most expansive vista of the Reservoir. The ridge continues south, forming Balsam Cap Mountain, and then falls onto the lower form of Hanover Mountain. Together, these mountains fronting the reservoir create a formation known as The Hand. The closed fist has summits for knuckles. Slide Mountain's summit rises behind The Hand.

An old road leads east from the pumphouses. The blocked road is now a 1.25 mile-walking trail. Under deteriorating concrete, the original brick shows through, enhancing the journey through space with one through time as well.

New York City takes more than 1.5 billion gallons of water each day from its water system. More than a third of it passes through the Ashokan Reservoir. Machinery and more than a hundred miles of pipe deliver this water, but the Catskills' heart is the holding tank. Once populated with small towns and farms, the lands beneath the reservoir now serve a common purpose.

The Ashokan's scenery is spectacular, but artificial. Man created this beauty. While the wisdom of the reservoir's construction is a matter of personal judgment, few engineering projects create the harmony found here. The reservoir's clean water supplies millions of people and saves billions of dollars, and despite the controversies surrounding local land use, the reservoir and the Catskill Mountain water it holds are among the biggest reasons the Catskills became a State Park and retain their wild nature.

MOUNT TREMPER

Hike: Mount Tremper
Roundtrip Hiking Distance: 5.8 miles
County and Town: Ulster, Shandaken
Parking: Along Old Route 28, between Mt. Tremper and
 Phoenicia (about 1.4 miles southeast of Phoenicia).
Difficulty: moderate
Bushwhack: no
Elevation Gain: 1900 feet

Mile: 0.0: Trail begins along Old Route 28, just southeast of
 Phoenicia (red markers).
 2.9: Summit of Tremper, return via same route.
 5.8: Return to trailhead.

Between Overlook Mountain and Ashokan High Point, the Catskills' eastern escarpment indents westward from the Hudson River. North of Overlook, the Great Wall of Manitou parallels the historic tidal river. South of Overlook, the wall collapses into a series of soft, low hills including Ohayo and Tonche Mountains. The escarpment then regains its stature with Ashokan High Point and Mombaccus Mountain. The Esopus Creek, which drains the central Catskills, flows through this gap between Overlook and Ashokan High Point. Mount Tremper marks the escarpment's deepest penetration. Despite being 25 miles west of the Catskills' eastern front, Mount Tremper resembles the escarpment's other mountains in its geology and ecology.

Named Oleberg by the Dutch, this 2,700-foot peak translates to "oil mountain." The oil refers to either the once-plentiful white walnuts pressed for oil, or the oily sheen found within the local rock. Oil shales are common throughout the Catskills.

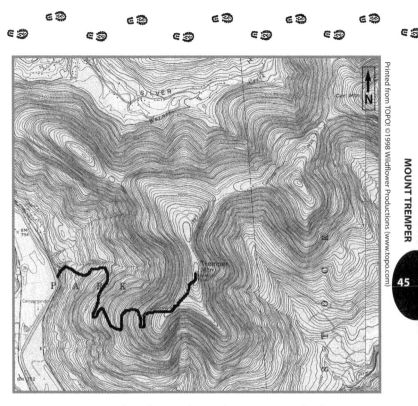

Mount Tremper's soft, southern slopes surround Phoenicia, a once-bustling Catskill town. Its proximity to the Esopus Valley, the major regional trading route, promoted Tremper's economic development. People cut the trees, burned the mountainside, and built roads and railroads along its slopes. Mount Tremper is still recovering from this intensive exploitation and it bears many scars.

In addition to a legacy of economic use unparalleled in the Catskills, Mount Tremper has a further distinction—it is the geographic center of the Catskills' high peaks. Mountain scenery from Tremper's summit is spectacular. The Catskills' highest summits rise west, north, south, and northeast of Tremper.

Trails to Tremper begin from its eastern and southern faces. The eastern approach is long and gentle. The southern trail is steeper and more direct, but makes for a pleasant journey filled with natural curiosities and signs of past economic use. The southern trail begins east of Phoenicia along the Esopus Creek's north shore. This section of the creek, Sleepy Hollow, is one of New York State's best trout waters. Its cold, clean water attract fish and fishermen.

The trail rises steeply from the streambank to crest a small ridge. Although the creek fades from view, the sound of its waters continue to spill over the landscape. Then the land levels, beginning a pattern continued throughout the hike: short, steep inclines and switchbacks connect long, flat stretches. The steep slopes tax muscles, but the level terraces leave energy for rest, contemplation, and enjoyment.

The wide, graded trail was a mountain road, one of many on Tremper. Timber companies built them in the 1800s, and bluestone quarriers also used them. Until recently, the State used this road to service the summit's fire tower.

A distinctive feature of Tremper is its young forest. Timber harvesting on Tremper was among the Catskills' most intensive. Hemlock stands provided tanbark, white pines became ship masts, and its hardwoods became fuel and building materials. A few decades later, the second generation saplings provided material for a barrel hoop industry. On Tremper, logging continued into the 20th century. Young regrowth and decaying stumps cover the mountain.

Forest fires also played a role in producing this young forest. Until the early 1920s, fires burned large areas of the sun-baked Catskills. Saplings could not retain adequate soil moisture, and the dry ground provided fuel for sparks, lightning, or carelessness to ignite. Fires have been uncommon since the forest cover returned, but between man's use and fire, few trees on Mount Tremper are more than 50 years old.

Mount Tremper's forests resemble Overlook Mountain's; trees less common to the Catskills dominate local forests here. White ash, northern red oak, yellow birch, and smaller numbers of black cherry, white pine, chestnut oak, American basswood, sugar maple, American beech, and red maple cover Tremper's slopes.

Hemlock, once dominant at this elevation, is absent from the canopy, but many saplings grow in the understory. Hemlocks grow

The view north from Tremper includes Slide, Wittenberg, and Cornell Mountains.

best in cool, damp environments. Direct sunlight and dry soils reduce hemlock's ability to survive. When forests first returned to Tremper's logged slopes, the oaks, ash, and pine prospered in the sunlight, while hemlock seedlings wilted and died; however, once these other species established themselves, they altered local microenvironments, reducing light, decreasing temperatures, and increasing soil moisture. Hemlock thrives in these conditions, confirmed by their feathery green foliage throughout the understory. Once established, few other plants can grow beneath a hemlock's shade.

After the existing canopy trees die, the hemlocks will grow into the openings, and, barring any large-scale disturbances, Mount Tremper's forests will revert to their former grandeur. In 250-300 years, mature hemlocks may again dominate many of these slopes, spreading their dark blue-green needles over the mountain. In contrast, today's deciduous forests cover Mount Tremper in a patchwork of medium greens.

Other signs of economic harvest line the trail. Near the trail's mid-point, a large, coarse rockpile looms above the natural landscape. Sculpted like a cheap imitation of the mountain, this rocky statue provides a stark contrast to the recovering forest. Its rocky, inferior construction supports only a few struggling trees and plants. The blocky pile is a memorial to man's influence on the environment and our limited success in restoring it. A side trail leads past this refuse to the quarry's center where Catskill bluestone, a major building material until the development of cement in the 1890s, was harvested.

The quarry's boundaries slice deep into the mountainside. The open rock, however, makes an excellent geologic profile. Each layer of bluestone represents a snapshot of the Earth's past. The Devonian shales, known for their ability to split into thin, flat planes, are more than 350 million years old. As stone masons and quarry workers cut this ancient stone, their geologic story became sidewalks in the United States' largest cities. Today, bluestone construction is a specialty based on nostalgia, but few people realize its Catskill origin.

Shallow soils, typical of the Catskills, cover the rock cut. The dark brown soils are full of rock and only a few inches thick. The resident plants must obtain nutrients and support from these thin soils. Blowdowns are common.

The quarry's open, sunny slopes make it a good place to find spring wildflowers and snakes. Early saxifrage, purple trillium, trout lilies, and spring beauties are among spring's harbingers. The sun-baked rock piles make an excellent snake habitat. Timber rattlers, one of the Catskills' two poisonous snakes, are common on Tremper's warm, dry slopes. Along with Overlook Mountain, Tremper shares the distinction of harboring the Catskills' largest timber rattler populations.

The main path reveals glimpses to the south as it continues to gain elevation. Tree skeletons break the scenes like stained glass windows. Slide Mountain, the Catskills' highest point, soars above the other peaks. From Slide's northern face, a ridge leads into the domed forms of Giant Ledge and Panther Mountain. The distinctive pinnacles of 3,780-foot Wittenberg and 3,860-foot Cornell Mountains are west of 4,180-foot Slide. Mount Pleasant's lower form rises across the Esopus Valley.

Forest composition changes on Tremper's higher elevations. Bent, twisted, and warped by high winds, the gnarled trees reflect the chaotic air currents. Branches rattle with each gust. Northern red oak dominates the forest, with lesser numbers of white pine, paper birch, yellow birch, black cherry, sugar maple, red maple, ironwood, and white ash. Hemlock remains in the understory. Beech become more common as elevation increases. An occasional big-tooth aspen, a pioneer species indicative of a young forest, also grows here. Large patches of mountain laurel grow beneath the oaks. In May and June, their waxy, pink and white flowers brighten the forest.

Till-derived soils and vegetation hide most of Tremper's native geologic surface. Only a few key features remain uncovered. Formations sculpted during the ice age outline the mountain's current shape. The trail's pattern of switchbacks and flat ridges result from stair-step topography. The trail often follows the flat ridges. Built like a layer cake, the Catskills' rock layers are horizontal and parallel. Strata shrink in area toward the summit. The sharp, horizontal layers resemble the Grand Canyon, but glaciation, high precipitation, and vegetation softened the Catskills.

The Wisconsin Ice sheet buried the Catskills in a mile-thick sea of ice. When the ice retreated 11,000 years ago, it dropped its sediment load as till. Mountaintops received small amounts of till, while valley floors received up to 200 feet. The Catskills' stair steps filled with till, smoothing the landscape. A few Catskill summits hold no till, but Tremper's small stature ensured complete burial.

Another glacial feature highlighting Mount Tremper is the large cirque shaping the mountain's southeastern face. When the Wisconsin Ice Sheet advanced into the Esopus Valley, it plowed into Mount Tremper and scoured its eastern slopes. The ice carved into the bedrock, changing the mountain's appearance. After the continental ice sheet retreated, alpine glaciers persisted in shaded scars. Ice accumulated and flowed down the hollows, further eroding the bedrock. The pool of ice and its outflow shaped the land into a cirque. When the climate warmed, the ice disappeared, but the landform remained. If the climate cools again, cirques will hold the region's first glaciers. Route 28 between Boiceville and Mount Tremper provides a good view of Mount Tremper's cirque.

Many hemlocks grow on the mountain's highest ridges. The higher elevation and east-facing slopes create cooler, moist conditions. Other environmental changes accompany this final ascent. Strong winds and winter ice stunt, bend, and break the trees, and many dead and dying trunks litter the mountaintop. Shrubs and grasses thrive in these canopy openings, their small stature sheltering them from the high winds. Beech trees dominate the moister soils, while pine-oak forests remain entrenched on the drier south-facing slopes. Red maples thrive without regard to local habitat differences. Together, the trees eclipse all potential vistas.

A rickety fire tower (closed to the public) stands atop Mount Tremper and provides an uncertain lift above the trees. Once free of the restrictive foliage, the tower reveals a dramatic 360-degree panorama. To the east, the Catskill Mountains contrast with the Hudson Valley. Olderbark, Indian Head, and Overlook Mountains are among the most prominent peaks. West of Tremper rise the Catskills' highest peaks, including Slide, Hunter, and Westkill Mountains. Smaller mountains fill the foreground, carved into their low forms by glaciers. Beautiful vistas open in all directions, but the gusty winds battering and shaking the tower often cut visits short.

The tower is a historic sentinel. Forest fires devastated the Catskills in the late 1800s and early 1900s. Before the use of airplanes and satellites, these towers were the primary defense against wildfires. Five towers, including Tremper's, still stand. Removal of these monuments would eliminate one of man's few positive influences on the Catskills. The towers, retired from their firefighting role, are beginning new careers as observation posts. In this capacity the towers educate and inspire, while reducing the need to cut mountaintop trees. Once restored the fire tower wil again allow the public to experience Tremper's grand vistas.

Man conquered Mount Tremper. Logged, and quarried, and subdued with roads and a tower, its pristine character left long ago. Today, Tremper recovers from this exploitation. Its slopes heal from wounds of past development. Mount Tremper is a tribute to mother nature's healing skills. Since it is easily accessible and has excellent vistas, this mountain will remain tame, but careful stewardship will also keep it wild.

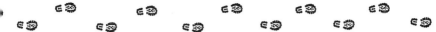

OVERLOOK MOUNTAIN

Hike: Overlook Mountain
Roundtrip Hiking Distance: 5.2 miles
County and Town: Ulster, Woodstock
Parking: Off Meads Mountain Road as it crests the saddle between Overlook and Guardian Mountains (across from Buddhist temple).
Difficulty: moderate
Bushwhack: no
Elevation Gain: 1400 feet

Mile: 0.0: Leave parking area in saddle between Overlook and Guardian Mountains.
1.1: Dirt road splits, take northern (left) fork.
1.8: Reach ruins of Overlook Mountain House.
1.9: Leave dirt road, heading south for escarpment trail.
2.6: Reach open ledges, turn back along dirt road.
2.7: Pass fire tower, continue back to parking area.
5.2: Return to parking area.

Overlook Mountain, sometimes called The Overlook, rises 3,150 feet above the Hudson River. Although an imposing form, it is not one of the Catskills' highest peaks. Despite its short stature, Overlook Mountain is among the Catskills' best known and distinctive peaks. Its appearance starkly contrasts with the placid river valley. Sharp ridges project from the uneven mountain into the calm lowlands. The Overlook's eastern slopes stand like a fortress wall. Set at the Catskill escarpment's southeastern limit, it is the Catskills' cornerstone. Local Indians identified it with the home of great spirits.

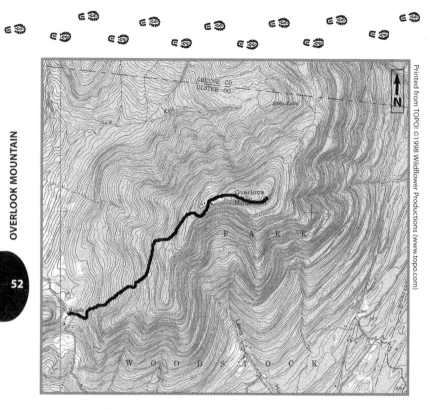

Overlook is the easternmost Catskill Mountain. When traveling up the Hudson River or the New York State Thruway, it is the first massif rising beyond the short, sharp Shawangunks. The Overlook makes an aggressive stand on the horizon, appearing as high as its neighbors. When closer to the mountain's slopes, its smaller stature becomes obvious, yet its strong profile still commands respect. The colorful town of Woodstock spreads along the mountain's southern base.

Overlook Mountain has a tradition of distinction, boasting landmarks of past and present. One of these structures, now in ruin, was to be a luxury hotel, while the other is a staple of modern communication. The monument to the mass media, a 300-foot tower scarring the mountain's skyline, stands out from every direction. In opposition with the Catskills' natural beauty, this metallic giant stings the mountain's forested profile like a slap to the face, providing a constant reminder of the cost of development. But sometimes a blemish enhances beauty, elicits a deeper appreciation for beauty, and hopefully the lifeless tower plays this role.

At the transmitter's base is the Overlook Mountain House's ruins. Completed in 1870, this Victorian structure became one of the Catskills' most prestigious hotels. For a short time, it was the favored vacation destination for America's high society. Known as the "summer white house" when President Ulysses S. Grant came for the favorable air, the Overlook Mountain House reigned supreme among the grand Catskill hotels. In 1875, this beautiful wooden structure burned to the ground. A larger, fancier wooden structure replaced it. The second Overlook Mountain House was 200 feet long, three stories tall, and had facilities for 150 guests. High winds atop the mountain required steel cables to anchor the structure.

Society largely ignored the Overlook Mountain House in its later years, and it became a sanitarium. In 1926, the second hotel burned to the ground. An attempt by the Newgold family to build a more permanent structure began in 1928, but the Great Depression's tight credit along with vandalism, theft, and World War II's call for manpower led to the project's abandonment. The state burned the decaying building in the 1960s, leaving a concrete skeleton. The silent, roofless halls await exploration and rediscovery. Preservation seems a wise choice for this lone monument to the Catskills' grand hotel era.

Although the trail leading from the saddle between Overlook and Guardian Mountains is unspectacular, the hike to Overlook's summit provides an invigorating experience. Once at the summit, breathtaking views compensate for the bland journey. Open ledges reveal vistas from the Palisades to Vermont. The Hudson Valley, central Catskills and Ashokan Reservoir dominate the vistas. The 132-billion-gallon reservoir is a blue gem sparkling in a sea of summer greenery. Slide Mountain rises in the west, its peak stretching 1,000 feet higher than The Overlook. The remainder of the Burroughs Range flanks Slide. Cooper Lake, Kingston's 1.2-billion-gallon water supply, nestles among the lower hills carving the western foreground.

A distinctive view fills the southwest. Three parallel, almost identical slopes rise from the Hudson Valley forming the Catskills' front. The closest ridge, South Mountain, begins its climb in the foreground, its slopes merging with Overlook Mountain's. A few miles farther southwest, another ridgeline begins. First it crests as Tonche Mountain, then falls into a small notch before rising to outline 2,500-foot Tycetonyk Mountain. A third, similarly shaped ridge lifts beyond the Ashokan Reservoir, climbing as the 3,098-foot Ashokan High Point. A natural curiosity, this parallel landscape resulted from the continental ice sheet's parallel intrusion. Opposed by similar rock layers, the ice carved similar topographical formations. On a smaller scale, such similarities occur throughout the Catskills, but this scene is among the Catskills' most impressive parallel formations.

The Overlook's ledges inspired paintings, literature, and exploration of the surrounding region. After visiting the Overlook's sandstone platforms, the beautiful vistas become one's personal inspiration. The contrast between the soft, rounded views to the east and

Looking west from the fire tower—the central Catskills.

south, and the rugged mountainous areas to the north and west enhance the scene.

An 80-foot metal-framed fire tower caps Overlook Mountain. It provides unobstructed views in all directions, revealing northern and western vistas hidden by the summit's pine oak forest. A trip up the creaky stairs tops the thick foliage. The wind picks up as the tower surges beyond the treetops. Stiff breezes sway the tower and bring a chill to the air. A few more steps complete the ascent, and a 360-degree view encircles the tower.

The Devil's Path Mountains trail to the northwest. These peaks appear Overlook's equal, but from atop any of them The Overlook falls away into proper perspective. Indian Head Mountain, the closest and lowest member, is 450 feet higher than Overlook Mountain. Twin, Sugarloaf, and Plateau complete this massive range. Olderbark Mountain springs from Plateau, its long, flat summit leading toward Cooper Lake's placid waters. A sliver of Westkill Mountain's 3,880-foot summit appears in the notch separating Plateau and Olderbark. To the north, isolated from other peaks, rise Kaaterskill High Peak and Roundtop. Beyond them is the Blackhead Range. In leafless seasons, the view along Overlook's spine is at its finest. The hotel ruins and broadcast tower contrast with one another and the surrounding wild forest.

The unique forests dressing Overlook Mountain are a mix of ecology and mystery. Man and nature both played roles in creating the current forest. Most Catskill forests, including Overlook's, are second growth. Valued for their hemlock trees, the Catskills' forests fed the region's thriving leather-tanning industry during the mid-1800s. Hemlock forests had begun growing 7,500 years ago, replacing a postglacial pine, spruce, and fir forest. The heavy logging eliminated many of the area's hemlock stands. One small grove lines the trail's lower section, its heavy shade reducing groundcover and muting sound.

Overlook Mountain's recovering forest, secluded slopes, and rich history create a tremendous floral diversity. While a typical northern hardwood forest, mainly American beech, sugar maple, and yellow birch, cover Overlook's northern slopes, its other faces are different.

Ruins of the never-completed Overlook Mountain House.

Northern red oak and chestnut oak join paper birch, white pine, yellow birch, and red spruce in composing Overlook's forests.

The Hudson Valley's proximity generates warmer temperatures on Overlook Mountain than are found on many other Catskill peaks. A strong southern exposure permits sunlight to melt snowpacks, dry soils, and further raise temperatures. When snowy scenes blanket neighboring mountains, The Overlook often remains a warmer brown. Except for the northwest slopes, where a northern hardwood forest dominates, the mountain escapes winter's coldest winds. Oaks grow better than northern hardwoods in the warm, dry conditions. Although warmer habitats promote faster decomposition, oak litter retains its structure and nutrients longer than other hardwoods.

Acorns require animals to move them, so oak trees expand their range slowly. Under natural conditions, the Overlook's warm, dry slopes would burn more often than surrounding terrain, preserving a habitat suitable for oak species. Thick bark protects chestnut oak's living tissues from light and moderate burns. Northern red oak also resists light burns. Since the early 1900s, however, fire suppression programs have allowed an understory of beech and red maple to develop beneath the oaks.

Overlook Mountain invites exploration. Wreckage from a small airplane rests below the mountain's first open ledge. When looking at the mangled plane, it is easy to imagine the forces involved when the speeding plane crashed into the forest. Gnarled wooden limbs bent and twisted as the aluminum craft lost its final battle with gravity. Extended wing flaps suggest the pilot's desperate attempt to avoid the fatal dive. The aluminum and titanium alloys littering the ground will record this fateful flight for generations to come.

Overlook Mountain's southern and eastern faces are excellent places to bushwhack. Since trails access only a small percentage of the Catskills, off-trail explorations are the only way to see most of the mountains. Seldom-visited lands and vistas provide extraordinary wilderness opportunities. To explore nature without a set path heightens the senses and requires good judgement at almost every turn.

While bushwhacking is difficult and sometimes dangerous, the rewards are worth the effort.

Off-trail exploration requires a good map and compass (or a GPS unit) and emergency supplies. Learning to bushwhack on Overlook Mountain has two major advantages. First, it is difficult to get lost on Overlook Mountain. Second, its slopes provide lots of adventure. The mountain's location makes it easy to remain oriented. The Hudson River, Kingston, Woodstock, the Ashokan Reservoir, or Overlook's summit—one of these landmarks is usually in view. If you do get lost, head toward any of these points and civilization is not far away. At night, nearby lights provide additional orientation. Deeper in the Catskills there are fewer landmarks, and it is easier to get lost.

Many spectacular views open from ledges throughout Overlook's upper elevations. Minister's Face, at 2,200 feet, is among the best. Rocky and foreboding, this 220-foot cliff-face is a huge gash on Overlook's eastern face. It is also a summer resort for snakes. Sun-warmed rocks provide great reptile habitat and rattlesnakes are common residents.

Along with the spectacular views from the summit, The Overlook's slopes hold adventure and history. As one of the first places to warm in the spring, and the last to cool in autumn, Overlook's extended season adds to its popularity. It is an easy destination for the beginning hiker, but it can challenge any explorer.

ASHOKAN HIGH POINT

Hike: Ashokan High Point
Roundtrip Hiking Distance: 7.6 miles
County and Town: Ulster, Olive
Parking: Off Peekamoose Road (County Route 42), 4.1 miles
south of intersection with State Route 28A in West Shokan.
Difficulty: moderate-difficult
Bushwhack: yes, .6 miles (roundtrip) from summit to eastern
viewpoint.
Elevation Gain: 1980 feet

Mile: 0.0: Trail begins along Peekamoose Road. Trail crosses
Kanape Brook.
1.6: Pass flat, open meadow.
2.7: Reach notch between Ashokan High Point and
Mombaccus Mountain. Turn north (left).
3.6: Summit of Ashokan High Point. Excellent viewpoint
located .3 miles to east-southeast (bushwhack).
3.8: Path continues west to various viewpoints. Return via
same route.
4.9: Return to notch between Ashokan High Point and
Mombaccus.
6.0: Pass meadow.
7.6: Return to parking area.

Ashokan High Point, officially named High Point, rises to an elevation of 3,098 feet. It is not one of the Catskills' highest summits, but its location along the Esopus Valley enhances its size. From most directions, High Point appears as the first towering peak at the end of a low, rolling plain. Like many peaks along the Catskills' eastern escarpment,

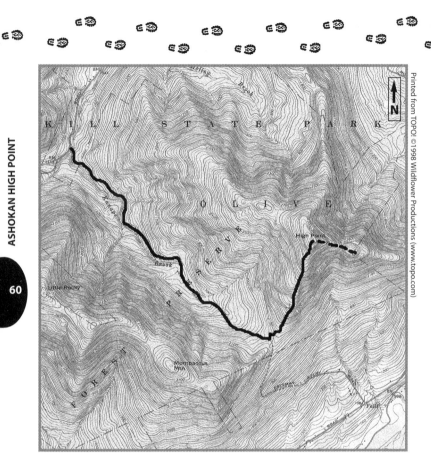

including Overlook and Tycetonyk Mountains, High Point's position magnifies its image. Rugged and distinctive, High Point's level summit and symmetrical side ridges make it a local landmark. A large gash on its eastern flank, Wagon Wheel Gap, is a curious landform with a rich natural and cultural history.

Indians never permanently settled the Catskills, but the mountains were a popular hunting ground. Except for an occasional trapper, Europeans avoided the foreboding mountains as well. High Point, because of its location near prime farmland, was one of the first mountains explored and used by European colonists. Wagon Wheel Gap, a large ravine on its eastern flank, was a Tory munitions dump during the Revolutionary War. Buttons and other Revolutionary War relics still wash from the ravine, but few other signs of this era remain.

A carriage road crossed the Catskills' escarpment on High Point's southern slopes, passing between it and Mombaccus Mountain. A direct but difficult route, this road cut travel time from Peekamoose to the lower Esopus Valley considerably. Quality construction marked this important transportation link. Bluestone lines the road's foundation. Hard-packed dirt and gravel knit to form a firm surface. It is no longer a major thoroughfare, but this carriage road survives as a trail. The trail traverses second-growth wilderness and the Catskills' eastern escarpment. It also provides access to High Point's summit.

The carriage road meets modern byways along Peekamoose Road. The trail to High Point begins between High Point and Little Rocky's western slopes. Immediately crossing Kanape Brook, the trail heads into reclaimed wilderness. Hemlocks line the cool, damp stream. The carriage trail heads east, following the lively waters upstream. The Kanape's tributaries draining High Point's southwestern slopes cross the trail before joining the main stream. Hand-constructed bridges, part of the old road, add a historic flavor. In use for a century and a half, many remain in excellent condition. Modern structures fortify other bridges victimized by floods and wear.

The trail's route passes through forests typical of the eastern Catskills, with sugar maple, red maple, beech, paper and yellow birch, northern red oak, and hemlock covering the land. Black cherry, white ash, chestnut oak, and white pine grow scattered about the forest, completing its inventory. Since High Point borders the Hudson Valley, many species common in the lowlands, especially oaks, are common here. More species grow at this geographical interface than deeper within the mountains. More than 20 tree species thrive on High Point's slopes.

Nestled between High Point and Little Rocky Mountains, the trail follows the Kanape Valley through a thriving second-growth forest. Small clearings speckle the landscape with sunlight. Halfway to the notch, the trail passes a sunny meadow where the Kanape lazily winds

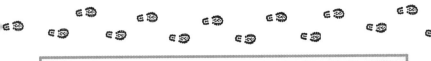

Peekamoose and Table Mountains from Ashokan High Point.

through the flat landscape, and an open canopy floods the area with light. Wildflowers, ferns, and grasses abound. Surrounded by northern hardwoods and dark conifers, the striking contrast makes this special place worth visiting.

After the meadow, the trail heads into a dense, foreboding stand of Norway spruce. Thick foliage gives the forest a quiet, eerie feeling. Long, purple-tinted cones litter the forest floor. A pungent spruce aroma drifts through the air. Many people use Norway spruce for Christmas trees. They also make good lawn trees since they have a long lifespan and retain their foliage.

Beyond the spruce grove, an older, larger northern hardwood forest dominates the slopes. Large beech, yellow birch, and northern red oak are the most abundant residents. The Kanape continues to diminish, and eventually strays from the trail. As it nears the notch, the trail becomes rocky and rutted. At the 2,050-foot saddle between High Point and Mombaccus Mountain, the carriage road intersects a trail heading north. The carriage road continues to the east, cresting the notch before its long descent into the Esopus Valley. A turn north leads to High Point's summit. Steeper than the carriage road, this trail climbs the remaining 1,030 feet in a mile, rivaling climbs to the Catskills' most difficult peaks.

Stunted trees accompany the slight lift onto High Point's exposed, dry, windswept southern shoulder. Most species growing below cannot survive in this hostile environment. Dominated by paper birch, chestnut oak, and northern red oak, the low forest resembles those of Mount Tremper and Overlook Mountain.

A large population of American chestnut trees live on the blocky, coarse-grained sandstone ledges. The shrubby, woody stems rarely top 15 feet, but they cover large areas. American chestnuts, once a major tree along the Catskills' eastern slopes, grew to 100 feet and more in height. Chestnuts were a major source of income for locals and a valuable wildlife food source. Chestnut blight, a disease introduced from China in 1904, killed every chestnut tree in the eastern United States. The chestnut's roots resist the blight and continue to produce viable sprouts, but blight spores find these young shoots and kill them within a few years. Research to control the blight continues, but at present the future of American chestnuts remains bleak. Nature may have better answers than man. A less aggressive strain of the fungal pathogen allows some chestnuts to reach 40 feet and produce nuts, so hope remains for the species' eventual recovery.

Without a solid canopy, the south-facing mountainside sits exposed to the elements. The direct sunlight quickly heats and dries the land. Soils crack and crumble, revealing the underlying bedrock. Winds batter the earth, twist trees, and evaporate soil moisture. When it rains, there is no overstory to soften the water's downward journey.

Worn by the elements, High Point's sandstone ledges are typical of the Catskills. Coarse-grained and light gray in color, these strata prove a match for erosion's minions. A thin, infertile soil tops the sandstone bedrock. As the glaciers retreated, they deposited unsorted tills, the raw materials for the region's soils. Transported from the north and east, most of these fragments came from nearby landforms. A small percentage migrated from the Adirondacks or beyond. As vegetation returned to the bare slopes, the till mixed with an organic layer to create the area's current soils.

Larger rocks decorate the ground, collecting near the small, exposed ledges. Broken off from local bedrock, the light gray sandstones and darker, weaker shales yielded to erosion and gravity. The Catskills' horizontal layering stands out where the path climbs the steep rock walls, the resistant sandstones protruding from the softer shale layers that undercut them. The unstable rock layers promote small rockslides along the ledges.

The trail repeats a pattern of short, steep inclines followed by level sections. Mombaccus Mountain's 2,800 feet escort the climb, providing a benchmark for determining elevation. High Point's summit appears unceremoniously. After cresting a final small ledge, the trail winds through a forest of dwarfed trees, blueberries, and hobblebush. Then, the land drops slightly and the path winds onto an exposed sandstone ledge. Three heavy bolts, once anchors for an observation tower, decorate the ledge. At first glance, the bolts resemble juncos, the tame white and gray birds common on High Point.

Ashokan High Point from the reservoir.

Even without the tower, the ledge reveals an extensive vista. Mombaccus Mountain continues its domination of the southwestern skyline. Across Rondout Creek's wide valley are the knife-edged Shawangunks. The Ashokan Reservoir fills the east and northeast. The rugged Devil's Path Mountains rise north of the reservoir. On clear days when the air is free of sulfur and humidity, this scene looks like a delicate painting. Subtle watercolor hues of blue blend to create the sky and water. Soft, textured greens and browns adorn the mountains, while a faint tint of warm reds touch the tree limbs as they strive for the sun.

Deer trails cover High Point's peak. One leads 100 yards west to a second open vista. The scene opens onto the region's highest peaks. Slide Mountain, 4,180 feet, tops them all. It towers well above the neighboring peaks: Peekamoose, Table, Lone, Rocky, Friday, Balsam Cap. Wittenberg and Cornell complete the view. All these peaks stand above 3,500 feet. Together, they compose the Catskills' geologic heart. As the thin trail descends to the northwest, it crosses open fields with additional views. Small waterholes are home to a large variety of frogs. Their eggs and tadpoles are common sights. The wider clearings, surrounded by low, windswept trees, provide a better view of Wittenberg and Cornell Mountains.

High Point's prize view sits a few hundred feet below the summit. Visible from the peak, this rocky platform tops the mountain's eastern profile. No distinct trail leads to the vista, so reaching it requires a short bushwhack. It is worth the extra effort. The direct route uses the summit and the viewpoint as landmarks. The rocky ledge opens into a stunning 270-degree panorama. Free of tree cover, the ledge provides views in every direction except for the west, which is blocked by High Point's looming mass. The sapphire waters of the Ashokan Reservoir appear to lap against High Point's lower slopes. On a clear day, the Devil's Path looks so vivid that one can almost seem to touch the finely sculpted peaks. Through the Devil's Path's notches rise peaks in the northern Catskills. To the southeast, the Shawangunks lead toward Ellenville and New Jersey.

High Point holds other rewards. A favorite are the blueberries. Low bush blueberries cover the mountain, and in late summer the mountain teems with sweet, ripe berries. The wildlife that eat them are also abundant. In past decades, people burned the mountain to encourage blueberry bush growth.

Autumn scenes from High Point are among the best in the eastern United States. With its extensive vistas, snack foods, and diverse terrain, High Point is one of the Catskills' most enjoyable summits any time of the year.

THE CENTRAL CATSKILLS

The Catskill's heart is Slide Mountain and its neighbors. The high mountains dominated by the Burroughs Range and Panther Mountain Circle hold some of the Catskills' most impressive sights. To ensure the popularity of the hotels along the Catskill escarpment, resort owners continued to call these peaks the "Shandaken Mountains" even after geologists determined that they were part of the same range as the escarpment. Now they reign as the Catskills' foremost peaks. Incredible views unfold from atop their summits, rivaling any in the eastern United States. Some of the peaks do not have trails, and the Catskills' largest wilderness looms within these depths. Major peaks of the central Catskills include Slide Mountain, Giant Ledge, Panther Mountain, a host of trailless peaks, and Cornell and Wittenberg Mountains.

The Devil's Path and balsam fir trees from Slide's summit.

SLIDE MOUNTAIN

Hike: Slide Mountain
Roundtrip Hiking Distance: 5.6 miles
County and Town: Ulster, Shandaken
Parking: Off Slide Mountain Road (County Route 47), .7 miles south of Winnisook Lake.
Difficulty: moderate-difficult
Bushwhack: no
Elevation Gain: 1700 feet

Mile: 0.0: Trail begins at parking area along County Route 47 after Winnisook Lake (yellow markers).
0.6: Trail merges with old road.
0.8: Turn east (left) onto Wittenberg-Cornell-Slide Trail (red markers).
2.2: Pass Curtis Ormsbee Trail on right. Views lie a small distance down the trail.
2.8: Summit of Slide, return via same route.
4.8: Return to yellow-marked trail. Turn north (right).
5.6: Return to parking area.

Slide Mountain, the Catskills' highest peak, soars to 4,180 feet. Its stalwart slopes rise 320 feet higher than its neighbors. Within the Appalachian Mountains, Slide is the first point north of Virginia's Old Stony Man to surpass 4,000 feet. Slide is also higher than many better-known Adirondack peaks.

Despite Slide's authority as the Catskills' highest point, it is hard to see. Closely packed within the central Catskills, surrounding peaks eclipse and shield its slopes. Seen from the Ashokan Reservoir, Slide's

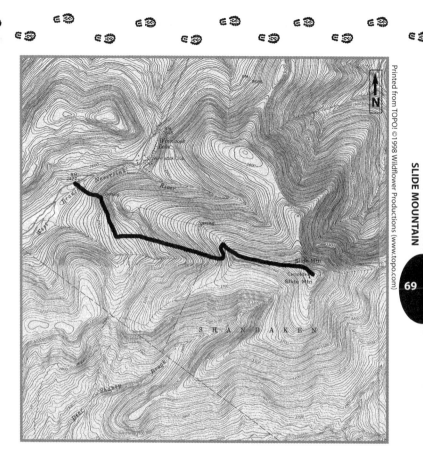

summit rises above the 3,500-foot ridge guarding its eastern slopes. Moving 30 miles to the east lifts Slide well above this ridge, but only a fraction of the giant mountain is visible. From the Taconic Mountains, 65 miles away, Slide's true stature finally towers above the central Catskills.

Slide Mountain's identity as the Catskills' highest peak did not emerge until the late 1800s. In 1879, Arnold Henry Guyot, a Swiss geographer, measured the Catskills' elevations using a simple barometer. The survey was the first to accurately appraise the region's summits. Since the Catskills' upper elevations were among the eastern

United States' most remote areas, Guyot's explorations were difficult. He often climbed into the forest canopy to determine location.

Guyot's careful technique resulted in elevations close to currently accepted values. Before his study, many Catskill elevations were educated guesses at best. Mountains once thought higher than Slide include 4,040-foot Hunter Mountain (second highest), 3,990-foot Black Dome Mountain (third), and long-term forerunner 3,655-foot Kaaterskill High Peak (twenty-first). Despite his precise work and excellent reputation, many people refused to acknowledge Slide as the Catskills' highest peak. Guyot's explorations and mapping efforts also influenced place names. Rusk Mountain, named for one of Guyot's guides, is one example.

Without a trail until the early 1900s, Slide Mountain was among the Catskills' most inaccessible places. Neighboring mountains and ridges prevent direct access, and Slide is a difficult climb. Naturalist John Burroughs popularized the mountain in his writings, and he was one of the few guides who led trips to the summit. Burroughs even conquered the Catskills' most difficult slope: a 1,200-foot landslide scarring Slide's northern face. The slide, inspiration for the mountain's name, occurred in the 1820s. Slide Mountain and its neighboring peaks along the Ashokan Reservoir compose the Burroughs Range, a memorial to the great naturalist. Among his works are essays and books fostering preservation of the Catskills and other natural areas.

Marked trails now ascend Slide's eastern, southwestern, and western faces. The easiest approach is from the west along the Wittenberg-Cornell-Slide Trail. The eastern half of the trail connects Cornell and Slide via a high, sharp ridge. Another route follows the Curtis Ormsbee Trail. When climbing Slide's western face, a short detour on the Ormsbee trail leads to a pair of south-facing vistas. The flat sandstone ledges provide excellent, sun-warmed viewing platforms. In the southwest rise VanWyck, Woodhull, Wildcat, Doubletop, Graham, Big Indian, Fir, and Eagle Mountains. Lifting from Slide's southern shoulders are Rocky, Lone, and Table Mountains. Balsam fir pierce the foreground and add to the depth of field. The dark evergreens also cap the distant summits. Unfortunately, the south-facing view often washes to gray as sulfur particles and harsh sunlight scatter the blue sky.

Rocks dominate the Slide's landscape. Strewn about the mountainside, the sandstone boulders pock and mottle the ground. Frequent freezing and thawing during colder climatic (periglacial) periods produced rivers of stone. Now, with the warmer climate, they appear frozen in time. The erosional process continues, but slow enough for soil to accumulate. Lichens and mosses grow on the rocky surfaces. Ferns and small trees live in the deeper soil pockets. If colder conditions return, this periglacial river will flow again as ice and water push the rocks downslope.

A classic Catskill forest of sugar maple, beech, and lesser numbers of yellow birch, black cherry, and hemlock dominate Slide's lower slopes. Striped maple and beech saplings hover in the understory. Small hemlocks line the cool, damp streamside habitats. The entire forest is second and third growth.

As the trail climbs the uneven terrain, the mountain's skeleton continues to control the land's character. Geology bests ecology for attention. Rocks, from pebbles to boulders, protrude everywhere. Unstable slopes produced the small landslides braiding the land. The trail often parallels or crosses rock-paved slopes and fields of jagged boulders.

The steep slopes quickly lift the trail into Slide's upper elevations. The northern hardwood forest grades into upper hardwoods and balsam fir. Once above 3,400 feet, white quartz pebbles pave the trail. The bright pathway resembles a garden walk. The quartz fragments, distinctive to Slide and its neighbors' higher elevations, readily crumble. The heavily weathered, even-sized grains decompose into a sandy, infertile soil. With its dark evergreens and clubmoss, the subalpine forest is a striking contrast of light and shadow. Feathery ferns and rough hobblebush leaves add texture. A chill touches the air year round, and the sound of scraping pebbles accompanies each step.

Before reaching the summit, a north-facing view pokes through a stand of balsam fir and yellow birch. The vista overlooks the domed summits of Giant Ledge and Panther Mountain. From this 3,500-foot perch, Panther Mountain's 3,720 feet pale in comparison with Slide's bulk. Giant Ledge and its 180-foot cliffs are well below this overlook. Farther north, Hunter, Plateau, Westkill, and Northdome Mountains form the horizon.

Slide's 4,180-foot summit is unique. Rising above its neighbors, it provides an exclusive perspective of the Catskills. A wide-ranging, east-facing vista opens from the summit's large, grassy clearing. The remainder of the Burroughs Range fills the foreground. The Ashokan Reservoir fills the Esopus basin, appearing as a shimmering blue crystal or cloaked in subdued grays. Further east, and 4,180 feet below this perch, the City of Kingston nestles against the Hudson River. Vermont's Green Mountains and the Berkshires of Massachusetts and Connecticut sculpt the eastern horizon.

The knife-edged Shawangunks hold the southeastern skyline. Skytop, a steadfast stone tower, caps a small knob, its gray tower jutting above the sharp cliffs. Bone-white, the resistant strata of the cliffs uphold the Shawangunks in its struggle against the elements. Below the watchful tower is Lake Mohonk and the Mohonk Mountain House, a resort rivaling and reminiscent of the great Catskills hotels of the late 1800s.

To the north, Westkill Mountain anchors the scene. The Devil's Path defines the northeastern sky, but its highest peaks are no match for Slide. Kaaterskill High Peak, Roundtop, and the Blackhead Range rise beyond the notches. The Catskills' eastern escarpment stands east of these rugged mountains, including its anchors of Overlook and Plattekill Mountains.

In the early 1900s, an observation tower topped Slide's dense stands of balsam fir. The tower's 360-degree panorama spied every Catskill summit exceeding 3,500 feet. No other Catskill peak boasted such a wide view. Now, the tower is part of history, but Slide's vistas still reveal most Catskill peaks above 3,500 feet.

Slide's summit has many distinctive features. Its bedrock is unique within the Catskills. The parallel horizontal rock layers that form the Catskills lie in the same relative positions in which they were deposited 350 million years ago. As a result, higher strata are younger than those below them; higher elevations are geologically younger than lower elevations. Being the Catskills' highest point, Slide's summit has the region's youngest rocks.

All of the sediments forming the Catskills were deposited as part of a series of massive river deltas during the Devonian Period. The area's sandstones are the youngest remnants of the Acadian Mountains. The next geological period, the Carboniferous, produced coal beds, and large coal formations lie west of the Poconos, Pennsylvania's equivalent of the Catskills. Slide's top rock strata resemble the sandstones and conglomerates directly beneath Pennsylvania's coal beds. If the Catskills were a few hundred feet higher, coal might cover the range, but any Catskill coal eroded millions of years ago.

Slide's summit receives more than 70 inches of annual precipitation, almost enough to classify it as rainforest. Much of it falls as snow, up to 200 inches per year. Clouds often stick to the mountaintop, soaking foliage and soil. The cool, moist environment supports a lush balsam fir forest, healthiest in the Catskills. In the eastern Catskills, balsam fir share the slopes with red spruce, but few spruce grow west of Cornell Mountain, a half-mile away. Elevation alone does not account for this distribution. Red spruce grow to 4,900 feet in the Adirondack's harsher climates. Soil conditions and land-use histories may play a role, but red spruce's range in the Catskills remains an ecological mystery.

Below Slide's summit, the rock platform peering east holds a plaque celebrating John Burroughs. The tribute rests near one of his favorite camping spots. This timeless ledge overlooks the spreading beauty of the Catskills' soft mountains and isolated valleys, a view rivaling any in the eastern United States.

Slide's protected location contributed to its lofty status. Recent glaciation produced powerful erosional episodes, but Slide escaped much of their fury. The most recent ice sheet, the Wisconsin, covered the Catskills except for Slide's summit. At the height of the advance, the Catskills were an icy sea with a single rocky island protruding from the lonely scene. Shielded from the rivers of ice, Slide watched them break on the neighboring peaks. When the ice retreated, Slide Mountain remained the highest ground. Any peaks higher than Slide lost their advantage during the glacial onslaught. If another ice sheet overruns the Catskills, this protection will continue, placing Slide even higher above the other Catskill peaks.

Slide Mountain, the grandest Catskill Mountain, is an awesome place, unique due to its higher elevations and cooler, wetter environment. It is the Catskills' highest peak and it reveals mountain scenery among the best in the eastern United States. Unlike its wild past, this accessible peak provides year round adventure.

GIANT LEDGE

Hike: Giant Ledge
Roundtrip Hiking Distance: 3.0 miles
County and Town: Ulster, Shandaken
Parking: Off Slide Mountain Road (County Route 47), 7.3 miles
    south of State Route 28.
Difficulty: moderate
Bushwhack: no
Elevation Gain: 1000 feet

Mile: 0.0: Trail begins at parking area along County Route 47 at
    sharp turn (yellow markers).
    0.7: Reach notch between Giant Ledge and Slide. Turn
    north (left, blue markers).
    1.5: Summit of Giant Ledge, views from eastern and
    western faces. Return via same route.
    2.3: Return to notch, turn west (right).
    3.0: Return to parking area.

Giant Ledge is one of the Catskills' easier hikes, and few places radiate the charm and character found atop this small peak. Accessible from all directions, this spectacular mountain presents many hiking opportunities. The trail tracing its main ridge looms over Woodland Valley and provides dramatic views of the surrounding central Catskills. The area's main route, the Giant Ledge-Panther Mountain-Fox Hollow Trail, follows a north-south bearing. South of Giant Ledge, a major junction merges trails from Slide Mountain, Woodland Valley, and nearby Slide Mountain Road. The trip from Woodland Valley is the most difficult; the path, an old town road, rises 2,300 feet in 2.5 miles. The northern approach via Fox Hollow includes a trip over Panther. A

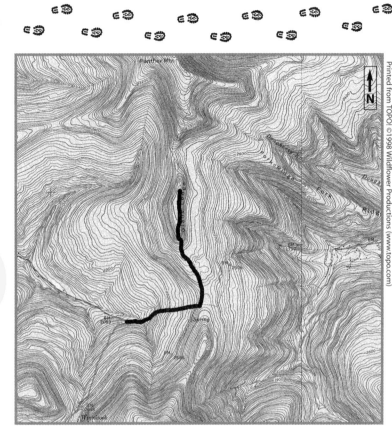

spur trail from Slide Mountain Road (Ulster County Route 47) provides the easiest and quickest access to Giant Ledge. When using this short route, ample time remains to explore and savor this magnificent area.

The trail begins at a small parking area along Slide Mountain Road. It plunges into the woods and quickly crosses two small streams. A small bridge tops the second, one of the Esopus Creek's headwaters. The creek is only a trickle here, but this mountain river grows as it gathers other small streams, and together they fill the Ashokan Reservoir. The water beneath this small bridge could soon flow from a New York City faucet. While the water continues its gravity-inspired journey, the path starts to ascend Giant Ledge.

The rocky trail begins its climb through a northern hardwood forest. Wooden columns of beech, sugar maple, yellow birch, black cherry, and hemlock thrust into the sky. The area's largest trees, healthy second growth forest, are 2 feet wide and 65 feet tall. Striped maple decorate the understory, along with a thick growth of ferns, oxalis, and mosses. Chipmunks dart through their secret maze of rounded boulders and underbrush. Cheery chickadees and subdued red-breasted nuthatches perch on nearby branches. Their songs fly through the air to mark territory and warn of danger.

Broken rocks cover the landscape, the result of almost continuous freezing and thawing episodes following the ice age. Splinters of bedrock cascaded down the mountain on a regular basis. As average temperature increased, freezes occurred less often and the process slowed; the boulders appear frozen in place. Along the trail, the rocks defining the route are bare, scraped clean by treading feet. In some places stone staircases define the footpath. Away from the trail, the rocks collect small pockets of soil that provide habitat for mosses, small animals, and resourceful trees. Hemlock and yellow birch are most common.

The trail maintains a steady climb until reaching the ridgetop. The four-way intersection is the mountain equivalent of an interstate highway cloverleaf. To the south lies Slide Mountain, while the eastern path leads to Woodland Valley. Giant Ledge is north. Within this protected notch, a forest of beech, hemlock, and black cherry clothe the land in silver, forest green, and black. Painted trillium, trout lilies, spring beauties, and assorted violets provide additional splashes of color. Autumn brings a different palette, as gold, orange, red, and yellow mix with the everyday forest attire.

Only 200 feet of elevation lift Giant Ledge from the notch. As the trail heads north, it follows a flat ridge. The poorly drained route is often waterlogged. Soft, dark soils and hard, gray sandstones play hopscotch in the trailbed. When saturated, the path degrades into a stagnant pond of black muck. A detour through the forest, while not good for the environment, can become the only sensible alternative. In some places, rock stepping stones make this choice unnecessary. Despite the wet conditions, the rich organic soil provides fair growing conditions. Communities of wildflowers, ferns, mosses, and trees thrive throughout this moist, upland habitat. Healthy stands of birch and cherry attest to the land's vigor despite heavy logging in the late 1800s.

A steep set of sandstone outcrops herald Giant Ledge's summit. The south-facing rocks warm rapidly when exposed to the sun. Talus slopes, littered with large, jagged rocks and boulders abut the outcrops' bases. The south-facing slopes also reveal partial views of Slide Mountain—its summit ridge covered by a dark cap of balsam fir. Slide's lower elevations vary from green to gold to brown, depending on the season. The twigs and branches of Giant Ledge's birch and cherry cut Slide's image into puzzle pieces. With a final swing east, the path rolls onto Giant Ledge's summit ridge.

Giant Ledge delivers as its name promises. It *is* a giant ledge. Its western face holds to the typical Catskill mold: a steep, rounded, glacially carved mountain. Giant Ledge's eastern face, however, is

Slide from Giant Ledge.

unique as its slopes turn vertical. The 180-foot cliff looms high above Woodland Valley and provides a series of panoramic ledges.

Since Giant Ledge's summit is less than 3,500 feet high, the DEC does not restrict camping to the winter season. Its easy access, beautiful vistas, and sheltering forests attract many outdoorsmen. As a result, overuse and abuse scar the flat mountaintop. Small pieces of garbage confetti the ground, and scores of fire rings blacken the area. Although these blemishes do not seriously threaten the ecosystem, they detract from this wilderness' charm, beauty, and definition. Giant Ledge is at the heart of a wilderness region. Designed to protect and preserve the Catskills' diversity, natural communities, and spectacular beauty, the wilderness designation balances use, access, and impact, but some places, like Giant Ledge, are being loved to death.

The forest topping Giant Ledge is a mixture of hardwoods and conifers. Striped maple, red maple, beech, mountain-ash, paper birch, yellow birch, and black cherry dominate the deciduous component. Red spruce, balsam fir, and a few hemlocks represent the evergreen population. Windy conditions bend, twist, and flag the trees. Most break, creating scraggly and dwarfed wooden sculptures. On most days, a gusty breeze continues the process.

Giant Ledge's vistas, among the Catskills' best, are its main attraction. The lone western view stems from a small rock outcrop. From there, the mountain drops into the Esopus Valley and then lifts onto the neighboring ridge. To the south, Slide Mountain dominates the skyline, but nearby vegetation partially eclipses it. Slide's northern and western ridges ring the head of the Esopus Valley. Winnisook Lake, nestled into Slide's western flank, marks the creek's source. The top of the ridge is the Esopus-Neversink divide. On the valley's west side, the uninterrupted range of Hemlock, Spruce, Fir, and Big Indian Mountains leads north from the divide. Big Indian rises directly west of the viewpoint. As the valley curves northwestward, the mountains follow. Eagle, Haynes, and Balsam Mountain continue the high ridge. Panther Mountain's shoulder blocks the remaining northern skyline. The western Catskills' highest peaks rise behind this ridge: 3,868-foot Graham and 3,860-foot Doubletop Mountains.

Giant Ledge's western view pales when compared with the extraordinary eastern vistas. Three factors create this spectacular panorama. First, the huge cliff provides a dramatic foreground. Second, the rugged depths of Woodland Valley contrast with surrounding mountains. And third, since the Esopus Valley lies more than 2,500 feet below the viewpoint, there is a tremendous difference in topography. These incredible vistas unfold atop a set of flat, exposed sandstone ledges. The sky is only one step away, and spruce, 80 feet tall, grow one long jump below the cliff. Across the Esopus Valley rises another set of high mountains. The charging roar of Woodland Valley Stream and Esopus Creek echo through the valley.

Slide Mountain's 4,180 feet again dominate the southern skyline. A ridge flows from Slide's steep eastern face to Cornell and Wittenberg Mountains. Together, these massive peaks compose the Catskills' largest mass. A large cirque carves a deep pocket between Cornell and Wittenberg.

Panther Mountain's eastern ridges rise a mile north of Giant Ledge. A set of low mountains sit between 3,720-foot Panther and 3,780-foot Wittenberg. Terrace and Cross Mountains begin the interlude from Wittenberg. Mount Pleasant and Romer Mountain meld with Panther's northern slopes. Although none of these peaks reach 3,000 feet, they make a pleasant scene; however, it is the picture frame they create that makes this view special.

The Esopus Valley provided man and nature with an easy access to the Catskills' interior. Rather than flowing over the northern Catskills, the continental ice sheets migrated up the Esopus Valley. As a result, glaciers heavily scoured the adjoining mountains. The ice sheets scratched, scraped, and eroded the local shales and sandstones. Composed of resistant rock, the mountains stalwartly withstood the erosional assault. In the end, when the ice retreated, the peaks along the Esopus Valley lost 900 feet more rock than their more protected northern and southern neighbors.

Within this ice-scoured picture frame are the northern Catskills' highest peaks. East of Panther's bulky slopes are Westkill Mountain's abrupt, flat-topped summit and Hunter's sprawling 4,040-foot peak. As this ridgeline, the Devil's Path, runs east, it defines Plateau, Sugarloaf, Twin, and Indian Head Mountains. Overlook and Plattekill, the latter's western slopes melding with Indian Head's, stand on the eastern escarpment. The entire scene appears like a detailed stone carving held at arms' length.

The northeastern foreground holds another collection of glacially worn mountains. Mount Tobias, Olderbark Mountain, and some unnamed peaks spill southwest from the Devil's Path. Kaaterskill High Peak fills the Devil's Path's Pecoy Notch. The scene is among the Catskills' most inspiring, and the savory vista makes the easy hike seem almost unfair.

Giant Ledge captures the Catskills' essence: wilderness, camping, wildlife, recreation, and awesome views, yet, unlike most Catskill wilderness areas, it lies within easy walking distance. It is a short trip that offers experiences more common to longer treks. Of all the places to visit in the Catskills, Giant Ledge rates among the best.

PANTHER MOUNTAIN

Hike: Panther Mountain
One-way Hiking Distance: 7.5 miles
County and Town: Ulster, Shandaken
Parking: Off Slide Mountain Road (County Route 47), 7.3 miles
    south of State Route 28 and at the southern end of Fox
    Hollow Road (off Route 28 in Shandaken).
Difficulty: moderate-difficult
Bushwhack: no
Elevation Gain: to Panther's summit–1620 feet; drop from
    Panther's summit to Fox Hollow–2300 feet.

(need 2 vehicles to complete trip via Fox Hollow)
Mile: 0.0: Trail begins at parking area along County Route 47 at
    sharp turn (yellow markers) and follows route to Giant
    Ledge. (See Giant Ledge, pages 75-76)
    1.5: Summit of Giant Ledge.
    2.0: Notch between Giant Ledge and Panther.
    3.3: Summit of Panther. Begin descent into Fox Hollow
    (can return by same route or Fox Hollow).
    6.9: Pass Fox Hollow lean-to.
    7.5: Reach Fox Hollow parking area.

Panther Mountain is an island of high elevation. The Esopus Valley encircles this 3,720-foot peak on three sides. An isthmus of ridgeline connects Panther to Slide Mountain's northern shoulder via Giant Ledge. Between Giant Ledge and Panther, the land falls into a 2,600-foot notch. This unique configuration spurs hearty geologic speculation. The rocks surrounding the Panther Mountain Circle all warp toward the summit. Is this uplifted circular mass random chance?

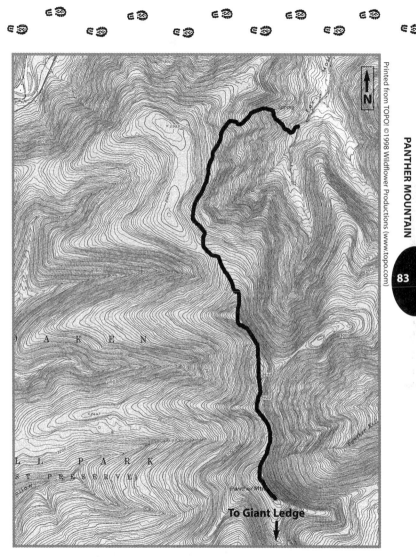

To Giant Ledge

Could it be the result of a meteorite impact? Or is it something completely different? Geologic surveys found that gravity is .2% lower in the circle than the Earth's average.

Panther's northeastern face is a large cirque. Ice lingered in this sheltered slope for 2,000 years after the Wisconsin Ice Sheet retreated northward. The mountain's large bowl-shaped cirque and steep topography resulted from the ice's erosional power. For more information about Panther Mountain's geologic past, see "A Brief Geologic History of the Catskills Mountains" at the beginning of the book.

Panther's sharp ridges create many false summits when ascending the mountain from Fox Hollow. Above 3,300 feet, a thick balsam fir forest dominates the summit. The dense vegetation eclipses the surrounding landscape and blankets the mountain with dark greens and fresh aromas. With its thick subalpine forest and past glaciation, Panther Mountain is a place of winter. It offers the most when the weather is cold and the trees sleep.

The climb to Panther's summit is easy. Its peak is a mile and a half beyond Giant Ledge, three miles from the trailhead. The trail is not steep. It connects the two mountains via a high ridge. After conquering Panther's summit, the trail descends into Fox Hollow. The additional access to Panther via Giant Ledge makes for a pleasant circuit hike.

After crossing Giant Ledge's summit, the trail winds down its northern face. Sandstone ledges bounce the path along the moderately steep incline. The rock's horizontal structure and crossbedding, a reflection of ancient river deltas, textures the mountain. A thin soil tops the coarse sandstones. Above them grow second and third growth forests of red spruce, black cherry, yellow birch, paper birch, hemlock, and beech. Hobblebush and striped maple dominate the understory. After the leaves fall in mid-October, the surrounding mountainscapes become visible. By early December, snow, ranging from powdery to crunchy, covers the landscape. Ice builds as people compact early season snows, so throughout the winter, ice-coated rocks will produce a slick and challenging route.

The path then shifts to the ridge's western face, revealing limited views of Balsam, Haynes, and Eagle Mountains' summits. A series of short descents and flat ledges bring the trail to the notch. Poor drainage, the aftermath of glacial scouring and till deposition, produces local soils best identified as mud, resulting in open, grassy terrain. Better-drained areas support second-growth forests of yellow birch, paper birch, black cherry, and beech, some of which reach impressive sizes. In time, this forest will mature into stands of thick, large trees with tops twisted and broken by the wind. Giant Ledge's northern face, sheltered from the sun's direct rays, remains cold throughout the winter, but as the trail emerges from Giant Ledge's mass, temperatures increase and the ice lessens it grip. Panther's southern flank further enhances this effect. The temperature on Panther's southern slopes are often 20F degrees warmer than Giant Ledge's northern face.

As the trail climbs Panther's sun-warmed slopes, it migrates to the ridge's eastern edge and immediately reveals a beautiful view. Framed by birch and cherry, the overlook scans a 180-degree panorama. A sharp drop provides additional perspective. In the southern foreground, slightly below eye level, is Giant Ledge's compact mass. Its eastern face juts over Woodland Valley. Exposed cliffs, gray and white, contrast with blue sky, green conifer stands, and earthy browns. On sunny winter days, ice-laden branches and rocks sparkle like a million diamonds.

To the south is Slide Mountain. East of Slide are Friday, Cornell, and Wittenberg Mountains, all higher than Panther except Friday. A large cirque sits between Cornell and Wittenberg. In the crisp winter air, sunlight and shadow stand in sharp opposition. Each ridge casts its silhouette on the neighboring mass, creating a patchwork of light and dark. To the north and northeast are the Devil's Path Mountains, and the northeastern foreground holds the lower peaks of Tremper, Pleasant, Tycetonyk, and Tobias. The Esopus and Woodland Valleys provide the area's deepest relief.

As the trail continues to climb, its course varies between steep slopes and wet, level ridges. Winter's ice can be a blessing compared with the swampy mess in these warmer sites. A look south reveals additional views of Slide Mountain. When the path returns to Panther's western side, it enters a balsam fir forest. The transition between forest types is quick. A few small firs mix with the hardwoods at 3,350 feet. By 3,450 feet, balsam fir dominates the forest. Unlike its eastern neighbors, few red spruce live on Panther Mountain.

At 3,500 feet, a meadow of grass and boulders opens along the trail. Despite the surrounding fir forest, the boulders are high enough to allow a view to the western Catskills' three highest peaks: Doubletop, Graham, and Balsam Lake Mountains. Each is easy to identify. Doubletop (3,860 feet) has twin, rounded summits. Graham's sharper summit rises eight feet higher than Doubletop. The lower, flatter ridgetop of Balsam Lake Mountain is farthest west, fifteen miles from Panther. A keen eye can see its fire tower.

Panther's final 200 feet of climb are gentle. Balsam fir, some more than a hundred years old and three feet in diameter, cover the mountaintop. Strong winds break exposed limbs and prune tree tops. Thousands of small fir trees huddle together and form a solid wall that provides a united front against winter's fury. Once the terrain levels, the slopes lose their southern exposure and temperatures quickly fall. Ice and snow again blanket the land, converting the trail into a skating rink.

Looking northeast from Panther at Wittenberg and Cornell.

Catskill conglomerate, the Catskill's most resistant rock, upholds Panther's summit. The dirty white rock contains rounded quartz stones cemented among a sand lattice. While this stone helps the Catskills defy the elements, in time it too will fail, and Panther Mountain will erode to its roots.

On the summit's northeastern edge, a rounded ledge competes with a lush fir stand to survey the northern horizon. Below the ledge is the deep cirque, the steep basin falling 3,000 feet into the Esopus Creek. North of the Esopus Valley are Halcott and Rose Mountains. A high ridge farther north sprouts Balsam, Sherill, and Northdome Mountains. After a deep notch, this ridge continues as West Westkill and Westkill Mountains. Rusk Mountain peeks through a point along the ridge. To the east, Hunter Mountain leads into Devil's Path: Plateau, Sugarloaf, Twin, and Indian Head Mountains. Stony Clove cleaves the land between Hunter and Plateau. Within this gap are the distant peaks of Black Dome, Thomas Cole, and Camels Hump. Kaaterskill High Peak's 3,655-foot summit fills the notch between Sugarloaf and Twin Mountains.

The return trip can either retrace the trail to Giant Ledge or follow the long descent into Fox Hollow. The route to Fox Hollow includes Panther Mountain's false summits. The deceiving landforms often trick people ascending Panther from Fox Hollow. Many return down the mountainside unaware they stopped short of the summit.

As the trail descends into Fox Hollow, the forest loses its subalpine character. First beech, then sugar maple and hemlock rejoin the forest. Many small streams parallel the trail, and winter freezes them in place and makes the route slick. Once among the lower elevations' sheltered slopes, the second-growth forest thrives. In spring, an understory of stinging nettles, colorful flowers, and feathery ferns complement the northern hardwoods. The trail ends as it enters Fox Hollow.

Panther Mountain provides good adventuring any time of year, but it is among the few mountains with great winter charm. Its attractions are best when the temperatures are worst. The climb up its southern face in winter is an enjoyable journey, and if the sun is out, it is even a relatively warm one.

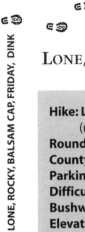

LONE, ROCKY, BALSAM CAP, FRIDAY, AND DINK

Hike: Lone, Rocky, Balsam Cap, Friday and Dink Mountains
   (not a recommended hike)
Roundtrip Hiking Distance: depends on route
County and Town: Ulster, Shandaken and Denning
Parking: Depends on route chosen.
Difficulty: extremely difficult
Bushwhack: yes
Elevation Gain: depends on route

(all trail-less—not a recommended hike)

Not every Catskill peak has trails created through man's toils. Some mountains capped in spruce and fir float in a tangled sea of obscurity. Isolated and shunned, these ominous wildernesses are thicker and tougher than trailside forests. Travel through these areas requires courage, curiosity, and endurance. Glimpses of beauty and thoughts of glory lose context among the hostile vegetation. Unconcerned with man's quest for adventure and knowledge, the dark woods engage in their own mortal competition for light, water, and nutrients.

Attempts to cross these mountaintops are a challenge to mind, body, and soul. Ice persists into June and returns in October. A landscape littered with cliffs, boulders, and holes characterizes the backcountry. Composure is hard to keep. Cliffs rise and fall without warning. With each passed tree, scratching and bruising, a nuisance at first, degrade into a painful debacle. Far-reaching vistas are hard to appreciate when each step tastes of pitch and wood. Spruce-fir forests thicker than prison bars triple the energy needed for each step.

In places, one must fight for every six inches of ground gained. After a time, intellectual curiosity yields to insect bites and stinging

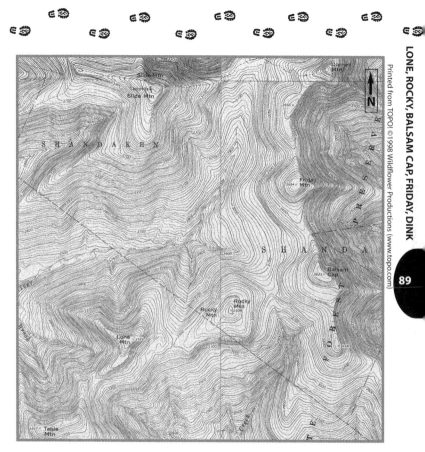

Printed from TOPO! ©1998 Wildflower Productions (www.topo.com)

vegetation. Memories form as feelings and generalities; specific images blend into a hazy record of the journey. For most hikers, the mountain allure is a mix of beautiful scenery and trailside wilderness, but miles from even a remote footpath, the untamed forests swallow these qualities whole. The quest of finding mountaintops without a trail is a challenge without equal.

Not every untamed peak is a difficult adventure, but most Catskill peaks above 3,500 feet are intensive hikes. Chaotic masses of young spruce-fir forest top most Catskill summits. Sprouted in the 1960s, these thriving stands replaced older spruce-fir cohorts. A few senior trees remain, but most died from old age, environmental stresses, or both. Elements of the spruce-fir forest play a large role in the off-trail wilderness experience. Soft balsam fir needles caress the skin, while spiny red spruce needles sting and prick without reprieve. In sheltered valley heads, a stubborn upper hardwood forest dominates the land. Between hobblebush's natural trip wires and interwoven birch and maple twigs, these areas are no easier to traverse.

Only a few people have the determination and stamina needed to explore these remote areas; even fewer choose to use it. West and southwest of the Ashokan Reservoir lies the Catskills' largest area without trails. A ridge, rarely falling below 3,300 feet, dominates the area between the reservoir, Slide Mountain, and Table Mountain. The trail to Table leads into this rugged terrain. From Table, a high ridge upholds Lone and Rocky Mountains before leading to Balsam Cap Mountain. Perched along the reservoir, the ridge surmounts Friday Mountain, then a small unnamed peak (unwittingly and informally called Dink Mountain by the author when first experienced), and then rises on to Cornell's upper slopes.

Table Mountain is a 3,847-foot, flat-topped peak. While the trail heads southeast for Peekamoose, a spur ridge heads northeast from the summit. After following the sharp ridge for a mile, it lifts onto 3,721-foot Lone Mountain. Vegetation changes as the land drops from Table Mountain. A stout, stunted upper hardwood forest, mainly yellow birch and black cherry, replaces the fir trees. Tall, dry grasses compress under the slightest pressure, the annual growth thriving between widely spaced trees. Trout lilies, spring beauties, and purple trillium highlight spring's greens.

The ridgetop is a thin strip of level land. Slopes among the Catskills' steepest drop to either side, but the ridge and its winding animal trails provide easy passage. Sheltered from the high winds, trees grow taller in the notch. Root systems, not leaf cover, limit tree growth. They must reach through thin, infertile, and excessively drained soils for nutrients, water, and support. Unimpaired by above-ground neighbors, tree crowns form spheres of twigs and leaves. The ridge is a peaceful place where an open sky spreads above this celestial platform. The virgin forest's sturdy, ancient trunks look as if they buttress the heavens. The ridgetop scene resembles a palace ballroom complete with high ceiling and regal atmosphere.

Rough rock outcrops provide a constant challenge while ascending Lone, but overall the climb is relatively easy. A look southeast reveals Table Mountain. Other small vistas open as elevation increases, but local vegetation eclipses most scenes. Once above the notch, fir again dominate the ecosystem. Frequent breezes stir the air and bring whiffs of aromatic balsam.

Lone's summit is a mix of meadow, tall fir stands, and stunted birch trees. The open space provides an easy, if not direct, route over the summit. Hemmed by complex weaves of birch leaves and fir needles, the mountaintop reveals no views. Lone's peak is business-like. Its natural processes proceed without human interference. The only sign of man is the Catskill 3500 Club's orange canister perched on a dead, gray fir. Its life-force gone, the large, slightly twisted trunk still reaches for the sunlight.

Rocky Mountain lies northeast of Lone, directly opposite Table. The distance to Rocky is about the same as that from Table to Lone, but this is the journey's only similarity. Lone's northeastern face, marked by 40-foot cliffs and dense fir stands, is difficult to descend. A comfortable, fairy-tale scene occupied the notch between Table and Lone. Similar hopes prevail when heading for Rocky, but never again do such pleasant, gentle forest communities grace this trailless expanse.

The forest's character changes while descending Lone. At first, the tree cover hints at easing, but thick stands of fir saplings soon pack the mountainside. Countless small fir trees create never-ending fence lines. Slender, stiff, and rough, dead branches slash and scrape one's unprotected limbs. The solid canopy reduces sunny days to dusk. Rusty, needle-covered ground, dark brown and gray tree bark, and green needles compose this inhospitable world. Cliffs, hidden in the dense vegetation, provide additional hazards. The setting is a claustrophobic nightmare. After falling, twisting, pushing, scraping, and climbing one's way down the mountainside, a notch ends the descent.

Rocky Mountain is the shortest member of the Catskill 3500 Club, but what the 3,508-foot mountain lacks in elevation, it compensates for with a difficult and, at times, impossible terrain. Like the short man with the big ego, Rocky Mountain makes a point of getting noticed, and it is a point well made.

Forest cover lessens in the notch between Lone and Rocky Mountains. Hardwoods mix with balsam fir, creating a brighter, more open community. Navigation is easier than on the descent. Mild slopes and open space allow rapid progress, but the easy passage quickly ends. First the land falls away from the ridge's sides, and the ridgetop steepens. Soon, the hardwoods give way to evergreen hordes, but not merely with soft, aromatic balsam fir needles. Red spruce joins the forest—its sharp, thin needles pricking unsuspecting flesh.

Isolated on a thin, rugged ridge, the painful journey to Rocky continues. The red spruce population increases with elevation. Before long, half the trees are spruce. Stings and pricks become more common

The Ashokan Reservoir from the gap separating Friday and Balsam Cap Mountains.

than heartbeats. The thick, tangled forest restricts movement. Often a fallen trunk will block a promising route. Over or back are the only options. To walk atop the fallen log is usually a dead end, yet some make temporary allies. They provide a few steps free from the forest's ensnaring tangle. Even then, the logs are a mixed blessing because getting off is another challenge. While one end lies on the ground, the other may rest ten feet above it. Positive thinking can be a major factor in soft landings when thick vegetation hides the ground.

Progress slows, measured not in miles, but feet. Specific location is difficult to pinpoint. Up is the only reliable guide among the overbearing forest. Most trees are less than five feet tall, providing glimpses of the intimidating landscape. Each new glance looks little different than past ones, but each one brings new hope of the summit. Each turns into a false hope. Stinging and grabbing increases with each step. The psychological toll begins to rival the physical one.

Finally, the land levels as the summit approaches. Dense vegetation covers the small, flat area. Until finding the Catskill 3500 Club's register, it is difficult to confirm the true peak. A clearing permits easier movement and reveals a limited view north, but Slide Mountain is the only landmark visible above the dense vegetation. The Catskills' highest peak, a lone beacon, is a welcome sight. After a few feet, the coniferous jungle returns, but an uplifted spirit provides the will to continue.

After cresting Rocky, the ridge continues northeast to Balsam Cap Mountain. It is a short, steep journey. A look toward this rounded peak brings an uplifting thought: Balsam Cap lines the Ashokan Reservoir, and this distinct feature remains nearby until the journey's end. The reservoir provides a good beacon in case one needs to exit the wilderness.

Steep cliffs quickly escort the land into the notch. The vegetation parts atop the cliffs, providing a needle-filled view of the Burroughs Range. Slide Mountain rises highest, a shepherd among the wilderness. East of Slide roam its flock: Cornell, Friday, and Balsam Cap. The eyes can easily trace the remaining journey, but the spent body remains unjubilant. Directly below awaits a steep descent through a thick spruce-fir forest.

Filled with cliffs, ledges, and trees, the descent from Rocky tests strength and agility. The land descends more than 300 feet in a quarter mile. The notch holds a mix of deciduous hardwoods, but their scraggly forms are not welcome in this coniferous wilderness. Red spruce now dominate the forest, their ever-present, sharp needles battering the senses. Water is hard to find along the route, despite 65 inches of annual precipitation. The thin soils drain too quickly. The notch provides one of the few places where water may collect. After a few steps in the tree-entombed notch, the land begins to rise.

The climb up Balsam Cap's western face is a steep and unyielding push. Spruce and sandstone compose the entire visible world, and it is easy to lose one's position among the wild forest. Small cliffs bar the way, but make a welcome diversion from the battering forest. The summit could lie over the next rise, but after Rocky's false summits, it is hard to tell. Fatigue builds, and careless hand placement can add a little blood to the price of treading in the wilderness. Like a child whose eyes are bigger than his stomach, ascending Balsam Cap looks easier than it is.

Balsam Cap's 3,643-foot peak arrives without the confusion surrounding Rocky's. When the land levels, the summit appears. The forest changes as yellow birch and paper birch accompany increasing numbers of balsam fir. Balsam Cap, however, does not remain true to its name. Only a few fir mix with the tangled collection of stunted birch, fire cherry, and hobblebush. Dried grasses fill the gaps between trees. Animal tracks cross the open peak. Balsam Cap's summit is an open, windblown, and uninviting place.

A few steps east of the summit, Balsam Cap compensates for the difficult climb. A scenic vista opens to the east and northeast. The Ashokan Reservoir dominates the view. It sparkles like a blue gem. Beyond the reservoir's northern shore rise the Devil's Path Mountains. Despite their name, the surrounding terrain is a greater hell. Cornell and Wittenberg's eastern slopes fill the northern foreground. Their steep, ice-scoured faces wall the reservoir's western shore. Balsam Cap's forests hide Friday Mountain, the next destination. Along the eastern horizon, the Hudson Valley and Taconic Hills' gentle terrain blend into an indistinct skyline.

Remote mountaintops like Balsam Cap remain untouched by man. The environment is much the same as it was 5,000 years ago. Winds and winter ice batter the spruce-fir forest, ferns, and dried grasses living on the summit. In the late 19th century, Arnold Henry Guyot, climbed these trailless peaks to determine their elevation. In his time, even the mountains' names were a source of confusion. Today's visitors experience the same isolation and wilderness experienced by generations of past explorers.

The drop toward Friday is uneventful. Dense stands of spruce and fir limit movement, but a determined effort produces progress. Where the trees are larger, small clearings make walking a little easier. Then, with one last sighting of Friday's summit, a dense forest returns to immerse the world in a dim sea of dark green.

Friday Mountain is the journey's last peak without a trail. North of it rises Cornell Mountain and its state-marked path. This inspiring thought fuels waning resolve. The notch between Friday and Balsam Cap comes quickly. Perhaps the slopes along the reservoir will provide a more open forest. Then, a few steps past the notch, the forest executes a

Lone and Table Mountains.

perfect ambush. The trees close in thicker than ever. Each tree must be pushed aside. Direct movement is impossible. Limbs of flesh entangle and snag on the wooden appendages. It is fortunate that wood breaks more easily than bone. The forest is oppressive, coating everything in evergreen. Huge downed trees block the route at random intervals. Some provide a balance beam of transportation, others are dead ends. Hope shatters and strength wanes with each passing step. Only the nearby steep drop leading to the reservoir's western shore provides orientation.

A move to the ridge's eastern edge holds a surprise. A trail springs from nowhere! The well-worn path starts as a small break in the solid mass of trees. The question is: how long will it last? With the trees relegated to lining the path, this trail feels like a smooth highway. The soft path, black from the organic soil, leads to a large clearing. The clearing's eastern edge opens to reveal one of the Catskills' best views.

The Ashokan Reservoir, a blue diamond among emerald mountains, dominates the scene. This isolated overlook is the Catskills' best view of the reservoir. Hunter, Plateau, Sugarloaf, Twin, Indian Head, Plattekill, and Overlook Mountains trail to the northeast. Overlook's 3,150 feet mold a sharp pinnacle, and it appears equal to its taller brothers. Tycetonyk and Ashokan High Point flank the reservoir's shores. A set of lower peaks, including Tobias, Tonche, Guardian, Ohayo and Olderbark, contour the land between the reservoir and the Devil's Path. The placid scene and imposing forest make a strong contrast. It challenges the mind to comprehend the savage forest and the ethereal view at the same time.

The trail's presence continues to keep spirits soaring as it heads toward Friday. Then, after a few yards, the path ends as abruptly as it began. The vegetative torture returns, accompanied by a steady climb. Pain replaces peace as branches rip at ears and eyes with a jealous intensity. Visibility falls to a few feet as evergreen needles fill every available space. Then, without warning, the trees part to reveal a huge cliff face.

Friday Mountain's massive cliffs dominate its southern face. Larger trees grow in the shelter provided by the imposing landform, opening the forest floor for easy travel. The 100-foot rock wall shows eternal patience as it defies man and the elements. Scraggly trees and numerous rock joints provide hand and foot holds and make the climb fun. The open slopes are a welcome change from the crowded forest. The 100 feet of climb are a nice boost toward the summit. A south-facing view from atop the cliff reveals Balsam Cap Mountain.

Once past the cliff, the tangled forest returns. Friday's summit is a low dome with no distinct peak. The true culmination is almost impossible to find. Occasional stands of giant red spruce loom over masses of short trees. Each is a potential beacon for the true summit, but all are false leads. Friday's summit forest is stunted to the point of ground-cover, sparing faces the torment of scratching branches. Still, the short, stout trees completely hide the ground, and ground-level branches constantly trip the careless on the uneven terrain.

Friday's northern face is a ferocious environment. The undergrowth remains thick and the view, while aesthetically pleasing, is psychologically oppressive. Small trees dominate the entire scene. No sign of man's world is visible. Cornell appears far away, and is no longer the next objective. A small peak, unnamed, but informally referred to as Dink Mountain, blocks progress. For an unrecognized mountain, the pile of rock appears imposing enough. Although not officially a distinct mountain, Dink stands between Cornell and Friday Mountains despite the insult.

The scene also poses a question: should the route bypass Dink Mountain and head directly for the trail on Cornell, or skirt Dink Mountain to reduce the climb? Or should the chosen path include conquering the unnamed mountain? After all, it *is* there.

Walls of forest make the decision to climb Dink Mountain easy. Movement heads toward the nameless peak by default. Even where the forest thins, steep slopes predetermine direction. Travel through the thinner vegetation is like wading though a pool of molasses and thorns. The vicious forest distributes pain with growing intensity. Since the force needed to penetrate the vegetation requires blind foot placement, each step is part challenge and part mystery. Hidden ledges lurk among the thick forest, revealed only after a leg slips over the edge. Progress means pain, and the only reward is more of the same.

Although not obvious from afar, Dink Mountain is a double peak. Cliffs on the southern peak's northern face are a complete surprise on the rounded summit. Large gaps open in the needle-hidden ground. The unannounced, camouflaged holes are among the forest's scariest places. A constant battering from the spruce-fir forest accompanies the new danger. Tree components work their way into clothing and attack every remote and private body part.

Dink's northern peak is only one more step in the wilderness, but it also marks the culmination of the forest's power. Trees stand more densely packed than sardines in a can. A short drop brings the land onto a level ridge with a partial vista of Cornell's looming mass. A tough climb still remains before reaching Cornell's summit, but at least it leads to a trail. Then, the forest opens and the trees get larger. Travel becomes easier, but the long journey has already sapped strength and tolerance. Spirited steps, some a little unsteady, come quicker as elevation increases. Torture and monotony give way to apprehension.

A line of light then penetrates the forest. Its radiance spreads through the forest floor. A set of rock outcrops come into sight. White pebbles trace the stone wall, an icon of the Catskills' higher elevations. On approaching the rocks and preparing for another climb, it becomes apparent that the white stones form a line. The darker forest returns after the bright intrusion. Spirits leap at the implication. This is the trail! No more tortuous forest! A few steps along the thoroughfare, a red trail marker confirms the route. The bushwhack is over. Lone, Rocky, Balsam Cap, Friday, and Dink Mountains stand conquered.

Cornell may have a trail, but 4.5 miles of that trail separate it from any road, and Wittenberg or Slide still remain between Cornell and civilization. But either path is easy compared to the trackless wilderness. Cornell's upper elevations provide an excellent view of the day's journey. Table Mountain, the ridge's other anchor, lies to the southwest. Between them are the soft slopes of Lone, steep Rocky, messy Balsam Cap, hellish Friday, and the supposedly unobtrusive, unnamed lump of Dink Mountain. With a few moments of contemplation, the eye easily traces the difficult route. After one last look, it is time to go home.

CORNELL AND WITTENBERG

Hike: Cornell and Wittenberg
Roundtrip Hiking Distance: 9.6 miles
County and Town: Ulster, Shandaken
Parking: At the end of Woodland Valley Road, just as it enters the State-run campsite.
Difficulty: difficult
Bushwhack: no
Elevation Gain: 2460 feet

Mile: 0.0: Trail begins by Woodland Valley campground and parking area.
2.6: Pass spur trail to Terrace Mountain.
3.9: Summit of Wittenberg.
4.2: Reach notch between Wittenberg and Cornell.
4.7: Short spur trail leads east (left) to Cornell's summit. Trail begins to descend.
4.8: Two excellent views. Retrace route to return.
5.7: Pass summit of Wittenberg.
9.6: Return to Woodland Valley and parking area.

Cornell and Wittenberg are two of the Catskills' most impressive peaks. Cornell's summit boasts 3,860 feet of elevation and is the Catskills' 9th highest peak. Wittenberg is 14th at 3,780 feet. Slide Mountain, west of Cornell, dwarfs both stalwart peaks, but both mountains lift more than 3,000 feet from their bases along the Ashokan Reservoir, and they are among the Catskills' tallest. Wittenberg holds another distinction. It is the Catskills' most massive mountain, commonly called The Wittenberg.

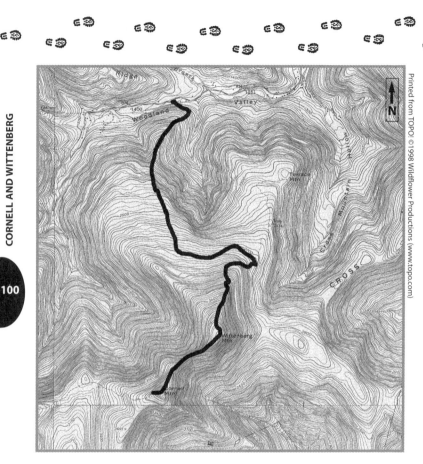

Past geographical confusion reversed Cornell and Friday Mountains on area maps. Among the Catskills' isolated high peaks, such uncertainty was common. Few people even attempted to climb Wittenberg and Cornell. Today, the journey remains difficult, but now a trail leads 3.9 miles from Woodland Valley to Wittenberg's summit. Cornell's crown is another half mile along the rugged trail.

The path to Wittenberg is unmercifully steep in some places, while nearly level in others. Filled with contrasts and curiosities, it is a challenge to any explorer. The rewards upon reaching Wittenberg's summit, however, are without equal in the Catskills. A spectacular 180-

degree vista opens from the peak. From this advantageous viewpoint, half the Catskills fill the horizon. In the northeast are the Devil's Path Mountains, with the smaller peaks of Tycetonyk, Tobias, and Tonche Mountains lining the Esopus Valley. Wittenberg's eastern slopes spill into the Ashokan Reservoir. Set among a verdant background, this blue pool dances with the mountains. Southeast of the reservoir rises 3,098-foot Ashokan High Point, and the slightly lower forms of Mombaccus and Little Rocky Mountains. The knife-edged Shawangunks slice the sky beyond these mountains. Capped by a hard, white quartzite, the Shawangunks' bleached cliffs gleam in the sunshine. Beyond these tilted mountains flows the majestic Hudson Valley. The Taconic Hills and Berkshire Mountains define the eastern horizon. Mt. Everett in southern Massachusetts, and Mt. Frisell, the highest point in Connecticut, stand out among the distant range.

The local setting enhances this incredible view. A natural amphitheater cradles the inviting scene. Lined with golden-hued sandstones, the grassy platform nestles into the mountaintop. Gentle breezes rattle the packed house of mountain-ash, yellow birch, spruce, and fir. It is a stage worthy of Broadway, and its show is awe inspiring.

Other views open along this mountain and justify the time and effort necessary to reach them. The scenic beauty of Cornell and Wittenberg often surpasses interpreting them with science. While technical pursuits bring new insights and perspectives, sometimes they distract from man's timeless relationship with nature. Directly using the senses, rather than employing them for data analysis, strengthens relationships often lost in the modern world. This story of Wittenberg and Cornell avoids the sciences in favor of a more sensory experience. It is this natural experience, the essence of the mountains, that is often lost to other interests. Only a little geologic history enhances the journey.

It is a late spring afternoon. Cornell's summit rises in the northeast hiding The Wittenberg from view. Slide Mountain's 4,180-foot pinnacle rises to the west. On the high ridge connecting Slide with Cornell, a trail descends the Catskills' highest peak. Steep and rugged, it stumbles among rocky cliffs. Progress is difficult. Saturated in a thick spruce-fir forest, the packed trees compete for sunlight and root space. Only along the trail does sunlight reach the ground. Occasionally, a dead tree's stark, bleached trunk breaks the dark green sea of subalpine forest. In sunlight, they become monuments to the ancient forest, the dead columns blazing beacons against the blue sky.

White stones line the steeply rising mountain pathway. Crushed and weathered quartz fragments provide this cobbled surface. Only a few other peaks hold this rare Catskill pavement, Slide and Table Mountains among them.

After completing another set of the unending twists and cliffs, the trail bends around a small outcrop and reveals a panoramic view. The view filling the western sky sits atop a flat sandstone cliff. Only a few slender maple and birch branches come between this overlook and the distant mountains.

Looking east from Wittenberg at Ashokan High Point, the Hudson Valley, and into Massachusetts and Connecticut.

Behind this chorus of branches rise a symphony of mountains. Rocky Mountain measures the view's southern limit. Sculpted into a small knob, Rocky is the lowest Catskill summit topping 3,500 feet. A high ridge connects it with 3,721-foot Lone and Table Mountains. Lone sits within Table's shadow. Peekamoose fills the background, its triangular peak cutting into the sky. Table and Peekamoose are the southeastern Catskills' highest peaks. Peekamoose reaches 3,843 feet and Table stretches four feet higher. To the west is 3,206-foot VanWyck Mountain. Its western slopes blend into Slide's rounded southern flank.

As the eye follows Slide Mountain's outline, it traces a north-south ridge. After Slide, the land falls into a deep notch, and then lifts onto Giant Ledge's soft contours. Once across its 180-foot cliffs, the land falls into another small notch. The ridge then rises onto the Panther Mountain Circle, cresting as Panther's 3,720-foot peak. Southwest of this high ridge are Balsam and Belleayre Mountains. Sherill and Balsam Mountains (yes, the Catskills have two Balsam Mountains!) lift north of Panther. The two peaks lead into Deep Notch. West of this deep gash rise Hanover, Halcott, and Vly Mountains, each more than 3,500 feet in elevation.

Continuing the climb, the trail comes to another lookout. From this perch, free of dense vegetation, the landscape opens again. The rock ledge reveals a wide vista toward the northern Catskills. Panther Mountain and Giant Ledge dominate the northwestern sky. To the north are the northwestern Catskills' highest peaks, Northdome and Sherill most distinctive among them. Westkill Mountain and 4,040-foot Hunter Mountain lift above Cornell's dense forests. Despite Hunter's stature, no white quartz layer adorns its summit.

From this overlook, a line drawn from peak to peak appears almost horizontal. Not a coincidence, this regional geologic feature relates to the rock structure. The scene evolved as erosion sculpted an uplifted plateau into mountains. Resistant sandstones atop the plateau maintain some of its original character. The Catskill Mountains grew down as ice, wind, and water deepened the valleys between the plateau's high points.

Dense vegetation covers Cornell's peak. Uncountable hordes of small trees call the mountaintop home. As the trail wanders through this subalpine jungle, it looks submerged in a sea of green, brown, and in winter, white. The actual summit lies beneath this tangle and passes without fanfare.

Soon the trail leaves Cornell's summit and descends into the notch separating Cornell and Wittenberg. Deep in shadow, the air cools as the mountain's western flank swallows the sun. An east-heading spur leads to a limited view of the Ashokan Reservoir and surrounding mountains. Trees obscure most of the reservoir and only a few peaks rise beyond the dense forest. Samuels Point guards the reservoir's northwestern tip, and on the northern shore, Tycetonyk Mountain rises 1,800 feet above the Catskills' base rock.

Evening's long shadows escort the path into the tangled notch. Steep drops characterize the trail, and the mountain walls drop the trail further

The Devil's Path from Wittenberg.

into darkness. Less than a half mile apart, Wittenberg and Cornell's peaks share similar profiles. Wittenberg's sun-highlighted outline lifts from the notch's northern slopes, its steep eastern face cloaked in shadow. A treeless cliff provides an unobstructed view north. Wittenberg dominates the foreground, and prominent summits throughout the northeastern Catskills hold the background. Farthest east is Overlook Mountain, rising from the Hudson Valley. North of Overlook is 3,100-foot Plattekill Mountain. The Devil's Path continues the skyline west of Plattekill. Indian Head, on its eastern end, shows its distinctive profile, while Plateau's long, flat summit anchors the range's western end. More distant peaks fill the notches along this rugged range. Kaaterskill High Peak's summit shows through Pecoy Notch, and the Blackhead Range fills Stony Clove. Hunter, traditionally part of the Devil's Path, is west of Stony Clove. Westkill's distinctive summit continues the Catskills' westward march, followed by Northdome, Sherill, Balsam, and Halcott Mountains.

The evening sun continues to recede from the sky and the land grows ever darker. Trailside vegetation are the only details still visible. The path reaches the notch connecting Cornell and Wittenberg while smothered within a thick spruce-fir forest. Dark silhouettes of balsam fir and red spruce form the border between black earth and white sky. Lighter shades become shadows, while dark colors become black holes. The ground is a mix of rusty needles and dark soils rich with decaying organic matter.

Glimpses of the Ashokan Reservoir open where the forest cover thins. The path then levels off, traverses the notch, and begins climbing the Catskills' most massive mountain. The trail, lost in twilight, keeps to the ridge's eastern face. Here, on Wittenberg's warmer, drier south-facing slopes, the vegetation changes. Spiny needles mix with the softer leaves of yellow birch and hobblebush. With vision fading, balsam's pungent odor seems stronger.

Shadows darken as evening marches into the Catskills, but the trail quickly tops Wittenberg, where stronger light adds definition. Deprived of Cornell's last 80 feet, Wittenberg lacks the crushed white quartz fragments. Instead, a coarse-grained, resistant sandstone covers Wittenberg's summit. At 3,780 feet, Wittenberg is not among the

Catskills' highest peaks, but its spectacular eastern vistas compensate for its lack of elevation.

Many people rate this view the Catskills' best, and among the most inspiring in the eastern United States. The evening backlighting enhances the scene. The sky's soft shades of blue blend with the mountain forests' pastel greens. In the view's center, the Ashokan Reservoir's blue waters also take on pastel hues, grading into the neighboring forest and sky.

After leaving this natural semicircular amphitheater, the trail quickly descends the mountain's western slopes. Woodland Valley lies 3.9 miles and 2,400 vertical feet below Wittenberg's summit. The trip down reverses one of the Catskills' most strenuous climbs. Since the

Looking north from Cornell at Wittenberg.

trail traverses the mountain's western half, the late-day sun has another chance to illuminate the trail. The subtle colors woven with indirect light on the eastern face yield to a harsh hierarchy of light and shadow. The evening light washes the western sky to a pale nothingness.

As the trail moves through the spruce-fir forest, it crosses layers of dark humus and light sandstone. After a quick drop along a series of small cliffs, the trail emerges into a northern hardwood forest. Sugar maple, red maple, striped maple, beech, and yellow birch form this common Catskill forest community. Fluffy, crisp, and fast decaying deciduous leaf litter replaces the spruce-fir forest's soft, rust-colored needle carpet. Although still thin, the soils here are a more even mix of mineral and organic components.

Color flees from the landscape as the day's final minutes sputter across the landscape. Then the sun sinks below Panther Mountain and is lost for the day. The diminishing light is adequate, but short-lived. Details wane with twilight's approach, and the trail becomes hard to follow. Only the bare rock, more common along the trail, helps distinguish the true path. Luckily, these lower, softer lands are easier to navigate than the mountaintop's steep, uncertain terrain.

Deer, typically active in late evening, feed in the peaceful atmosphere. As the light fades, pupils widen to provide additional light. The darkness thickens as the trail passes through small hemlock groves. The path becomes almost impossible to follow without artificial light. Cool, damp places, the groves cast heavy shadows during the day and become tunnels of blackness at twilight. An eerie silence turns the hemlock grove into an oppressive stand.

With dusk surrendering to full darkness, the trail makes its final approach into Woodland Valley. Lights and sounds from the isolated clove drift up the mountainside. The stream grows from a soft murmur to a stereophonic roar, and the air grows damp with its moisture. A steep decline marks the final descent where a bridge spans Woodland Valley Stream. Upon crossing the rushing waters, both the trail and the day draw to a close.

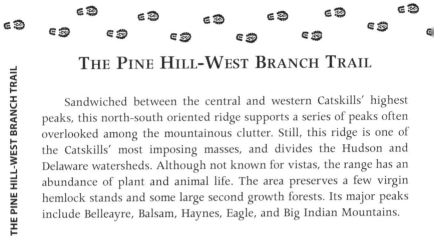

THE PINE HILL-WEST BRANCH TRAIL

Sandwiched between the central and western Catskills' highest peaks, this north-south oriented ridge supports a series of peaks often overlooked among the mountainous clutter. Still, this ridge is one of the Catskills' most imposing masses, and divides the Hudson and Delaware watersheds. Although not known for vistas, the range has an abundance of plant and animal life. The area preserves a few virgin hemlock stands and some large second growth forests. Its major peaks include Belleayre, Balsam, Haynes, Eagle, and Big Indian Mountains.

The view north from Belleayre—Bearpen and Vly Mountains.

BELLEAYRE MOUNTAIN

Hike: Belleayre Mountain
Roundtrip Hiking Distance: 6.3 miles
County and Town: Ulster, Shandaken
Parking: Off Mill Street (via Main Street and Bonnie View Road) in Pine Hill.
Difficulty: moderate-difficult
Bushwhack: no
Elevation Gain: 1780 feet

Mile: 0.0: Begin by following railroad track west off Pine Hill's Mill Street.

0.5: Turn south onto Cathedral Glen Trail (blue markers).

1.2: Meet up with ski trail.

1.6: Leave ski trail, head east.

1.8: Junction with Belleayre Ridge Trail (red markers). Turn west.

2.5: Reach top of ski area. Return east on Belleayre Ridge Trail.

3.5: Belleayre's summit. Turn north on Pine Hill-West Branch Trail (blue markers).

6.3: Return to Pine Hill, follow old railroad bed west to parking area.

The Ulster-Delaware County boundary also separates the hardest Catskill sandstones from weaker strata. To the east, in Ulster County, lift the Catskill's highest summits. To the west, softer hills blend into the Allegheny Plateau. East of this boundary, along the central Catskills' major pass, stands Belleayre Mountain. At 3,420 feet, Belleayre rises above Delaware County's hills, but sits in the shadow of its Ulster County neighbors.

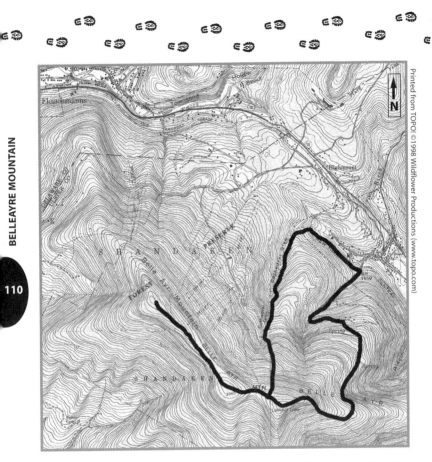

Belleayre's location along a major transportation route led to its exploitation. Extensively logged in the 1800s, the practice still continues on its lower slopes. In this recreational age, two ski areas carve the mountain's northern slopes, and hiking and cross-country ski trails cover the mountain. Despite these impacts, Belleayre invites exploration. Its calm, peaceful forests share the slopes with trail and traveler.

Many trails lead to Belleayre's long, flat summit. One scenic route begins near Pine Hill and rises through Cathedral Glen to the main ridge. Appropriate for this man-tamed mountain, the trek begins along abandoned railroad tracks. Part of the Delaware and Hudson Line, this was once a major Catskill travel artery. The defunct line slices through the recovering forest, but restoration efforts may save this historic railway.

Cleared, subdued, and maintained for a century, this land shows signs of past abuses. Soil compaction and man's continued clearing prevented trees from growing on or near the tracks. Even the surrounding forest is less than 40 years old, dominated by sun-loving pioneers. A few small quaking aspen, gray birch, and white ash grow on the tracks. When in season, blackberries, raspberries, and strawberries attract wildlife, and wildflowers abound along the sun-drenched railway. Summer blooms include Queen Anne's lace, pinks, healall, oxeye daisy, white clover, purple clover, and yellow wood sorrel.

The forest's edge melds field and wood. Ferns proliferate along this boundary. The forest holds primarily northern hardwoods. Their shade cools the air and retains moisture.

A small artificial pond marks the foot-trail's departure from the railroad tracks. The pond is a water reserve for snowmaking. Its brown, muddy water is a result of heavy erosion. Until neighboring slopes moderate, the erosion will continue. Eventually, vegetation will stabilize this man-altered land.

While the decaying, rusty tracks continue into Delaware County, the path climbs the pond's eastern shore. The old field escorting the railroad yields to a hemlock-northern hardwood forest. Shade replaces sun, relocating the sky beyond a dense cover of needles and leaves. The thick forest moderates breezes, stilling the air. A small stream trickles along a rocky course. Hemlocks line the stream while beech and white pine compete for the light and nutrients on surrounding slopes.

The forest's recovery shows setbacks on the beeches' graceful gray trunks. Beech bark disease, caused by a small insect and subsequent fungal attack, is often fatal. Symptoms are easy to spot. Beech bark, normally smooth, becomes pocked, cracked, and raised. White, wax-coated beech scales feed on healthy and diseased trees. The fungus' red spores reveal the disease's progression.

Beech bark disease is a disease complex, meaning that more than one event must occur to cause the malady. The steps must happen in a specific order to cause infection. Trees can have single elements of the disease without full development. In a case of beech bark disease, the beech scale, an insect, feeds on sap. The scale secretes a chemical to prevent the tree from closing this feeding hole, thus assuring a constant food supply, but the secretion impairs the beeches' natural defense mechanisms that normally fight fungal attacks. Spores from nectria fungus are spread by the wind and can settle into these untreated injuries. Undetected because of the beech scale's secretions, the fungus grows unchecked. The tree cannot respond until it is too late. The nectria fungus predisposes the tree to further infection and rot. Within a few years, the fungus spreads, killing the tree via girdling—the elimination of transport between leaves and roots—or rot. Often another fungus, *Armillaria*, attacks weakened trees suffering environmental stress. *Armillaria*, present in most soils, rarely attacks healthy trees.

The trail remains parallel with the small stream, but the forest changes as the slope steepens. Dark green hemlock needles dominate the woods, shrouding the landscape in shade. Hemlocks prefer cool, damp conditions, and often grow near streams. The northern hardwoods' brighter foliage cannot penetrate the hemlock's dim refuge. The soft, thick, and unrelenting shade cools the air and creates a muted, dark, and humid forest. Most of these hemlocks are young or middle aged, since loggers spared few of the Catskills' large trees.

Where old-growth hemlocks did escape cutting, the forest retains an ancient character. Huge wooden columns support a lacy evergreen ceiling. Beyond it, the sky's blue dome blazes in the sun's glory. This ethereal place is Cathedral Glen. Huge, old-growth hemlocks reach into the heavens, while the smaller trees compose another generation of the faithful. The glen is a cool, dark haven from summer's heat, and a shield from winter's cold and wind. The hemlocks along the trail create an interwoven tunnel of needles.

Slopes continue to steepen as the trail moves through the hemlock forest. Dense shade excludes sunlight, and few ground plants can grow beneath a hemlock stand. Instead, brown needles carpet the forest floor, a storehouse for nutrients from past years' growth. Slowly, this carpet decays into new soil.

The return of deciduous leaves marks the end of Cathedral Glen. Yellow birch, beech, and sugar maple leaves blend with dark hemlock needles. The mixed greens produce a forest of highlight and shadow, a common local theme.

The V-shaped valley holds a youthful stream, existing only since the Wisconsin Ice Sheet's retreat 11,000 years ago. Particles eroded from Belleayre Mountain flow into the Esopus basin and then into the Hudson River. After they reach New York Harbor, the sediments settle into the Atlantic Ocean.

The wide trail was once a logging road. Trees ten feet in diameter and 200 feet tall left the forest via this route. Large-scale logging continued in the Catskills well into the 20th century, and private landowners still log and develop sections of Belleayre. A complex network of trails and dirt roads, many half-forgotten and overgrown, cover this domesticated mountain.

More small hemlock stands yield to a mixed northern hardwood forest. White ash, northern red oak, striped maple, beech, yellow birch, and sugar maple share the slopes with hemlock. Understory vegetation is densest along the path, where more light can penetrate the canopy. Thick patches of wood sorrel, saplings, and ferns live in the brighter conditions. The sorrel blooms in midsummer, speckling the forest floor in purple and white. Purple and painted trillium grow among the sorrel patches, displaying their sets of three leaves and petals, or single seedpods. Ground spruce, a clubmoss, lives in the moister microenvironments.

Signs of beech bark disease are prevalent, its long-term effects visible among stands of gnarled, twisted, and deformed beech trees. Since the disease does not kill root systems, new trees sprout from healthy root stock, and saplings grow rapidly in the sun-filled understory. Within a decade the beech scale, and then the fungus, again colonize the saplings. Each infection site creates a pock. The disease continuously weakens the struggling trees, creating a scarred and cratered trunk. Soon, the young beech begins to rot, and *Armillaria* attacks the weakened tree. Often more black than gray, the malformed tree either collapses or loses the ability to transport materials. The disease in these later generations follows a different cycle than mature trees hit with the initial infection, but the result is the same.

Local plants must obtain nutrients and support from the thin, rocky soils. Belleayre's soils evolved from glacial till and organic material. The till, now weathering into sand and silt, covers the entire mountain, but is thicker on lower slopes. When the Wisconsin Ice Sheet retreated from the area 11,000 years ago, a new soil had to form. The reddish-brown, shallow, sandy loam inceptisol is full of gravel and small rocks. Its fertility is moderate, but limited by a low volume of material.

Gray sandstones, derived from ancient river bank deposits, are a common mountainside covering. Each crossbedded layer represents a sandbar from a nameless river's history. As with modern rivers, sandbars migrate. If buried, they can become sediment layers. The Catskills sandstones preserve buried sandbars and small fossil fragments from 350 million years ago.

Like frosting on a cake, a few rounded boulders pepper the forest. The exposed rocks' distribution relates to the area's glaciation. Some are erratics, transported from another region, such as the Adirondacks, but most came from local bedrock.

The trail maintains its steady upward journey, and the forest continues to change. Small northern hardwoods and a dense understory dominate the recently logged slopes. Hemlocks monopolize the streambank. Their deep shade and the bare understory strongly contrast with the verdant hardwood undergrowth. Chipmunks dart through the streamside rocks and vegetation, merrily chirping as they work.

The well-defined trail abruptly ends at an old ski trail. The forest yields to a sea of ferns. The route climbs this sunny, exposed slope. Wind-driven waves glide across the ferns to create a shimmering landscape of soft green. Gentle fronds brush the skin without pause. A sharp boundary of trees surrounds the cleared area, awaiting the opportunity to colonize the open slopes. Although the change in environment provides a unique distraction, the snaking path becomes steep and monotonous, and the sun, no longer hidden beyond a forest canopy, heats the air and one's body.

After sailing the fern sea, the path returns to the forest. The fantasy landscape fades from view, but not from memory. Black cherry, beech, yellow birch, sugar maple, and striped maple compose the forest. Another short climb delivers the trail to Belleayre's top ridge where a fire tower once stood on the eastern summit. Current views depend on the cleared ski trails to the west. The ridgetop trail holds a dirt service road. In summer, the open roadside holds a garden of sweet and juicy wild strawberries and blueberries.

Belleayre's true peak lies near the ski center. The area's widest views peer northward. Despite the ski slopes, lifts, and light poles, the surrounding mountainscape is an enjoyable scene. To the west, the landscape fills with Delaware County's endless hills. Plattekill Mountain at 3,375 feet is highest among them. North of Belleayre is Halcott Mountain. Rose Mountain sits east of Halcott, bounded by the concrete scar of Route 28. Vly rises behind Rose, followed by Bearpen Mountain's 3,600-foot summit. Deep Clove separates Vly and Halcott from Sherill and Northdome Mountains. Westkill and Hunter Mountains highlight the northeastern skyline. Mt. Tremper fills the eastern foreground, and the Devil's Path Mountains fill in behind it. Overlook and Plattekill Mountains (the Catskills have two Plattekill Mountains) define the eastern horizon.

Beyond the small ski lodge's generous wooden deck, a small clearing looks south toward Balsam Lake Mountain. A fire tower juts above its flat summit. Graham Mountain is Balsam Lake Mountain's eastern neighbor. The ruins of its old television relay station poke into the sky. Dry Brook Ridge lies to the southwest.

The ski trails carve Belleayre's northeastern face and head for the main lodge. From there, paved roads complete a trip down the mountain. Backtracking along the service road leads to a clearing one mile east of the ski center. This is Belleayre's eastern summit (3,380 feet), and a major trail junction. Any of these trails provides an enjoyable route, and all of them convey the mountain's comfortable, tamed atmosphere.

BALSAM MOUNTAIN

Hike: Balsam Mountain
Roundtrip Hiking Distance: 5.0 miles
County and Town: Ulster, Shandaken and Hardenburgh
Parking: At the end of Rider Hollow Road (accessible via Ulster
County Route 49A).
Difficulty: moderate-difficult
Bushwhack: no
Elevation Gain: 1600 feet

Mile: 0.0: Trail starts along Rider Hollow Road (red markers).
0.3: Pass lean-to.
1.6: Reach notch and junction with Pine Hill-West Branch
Trail (blue markers). Turn north.
2.3: Summit of Balsam Mountain.
3.6: Junction with Mine Hollow Trail (yellow markers).
Turn west.
4.6: Rejoin Oliveria-Mapledale Trail. Turn west.
5.0: Return to Rider Hollow Road.

Balsam Mountain rises in the western Catskills, its 3,600-foot summit among the Catskills' 35 highest peaks. Its winter beauty makes Balsam a required winter hike of the Catskill 3500 Club. Its high ridges sport few panoramic views, but its limited overlooks and lush environment are a rewarding trip. Balsam's location, near a major Catskill thoroughfare (State Route 28), provides easy access, while its varied natural communities provide a diverse look at the Catskills' natural history.

Balsam Mountain's most distinct feature is its undisturbed environment. Although not virgin forest, its slopes offer sanctuary from

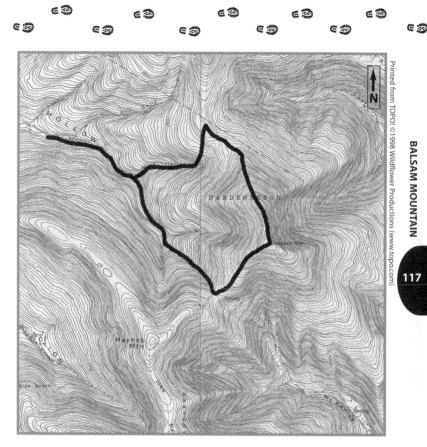

civilization. The unspoiled wilderness is a healthy wildlife habitat with diverse flora and fauna. Bird and mammal populations thrive, and signs of their presence are common.

Timber companies cut most of the region's trees in the mid-1800s to provide tanbark for the leather industry. Free from man's direct impacts since the late 1800s, the regenerating forest reveals few signs of the past intrusions. By the mid-1900s, forests reclaimed Balsam Mountain. Plant diversity ranges from ancient hemlock groves to large colonies of foamflower. Maple, beech, oak, ash, and hemlock shade the ground as the trail ascends 1,700 feet from valley forest to mountain summit. The privately owned summit prohibits hunting, fishing, trapping, and other high-impact activities, providing additional protection for wildlife.

Balsam's trails receive less use than other areas of the Catskills. Few human footprints mark the route, and mossy brooks play with the path as they flow down the mountain. Unobtrusive and easily lost, the path is usually a small dirt ribbon rarely reaching a foot in width. Ferns and flowers meander into the little-used path, and wildlife is never far away.

Deer frequent Balsam's slopes. Thousands live in the Catskills now, more than at any time in the past. With the elimination of their predators, such as the gray wolf, and the creation of large grazing areas, deer populations soared. Hunting, disease, and hunger are the only viable population controls remaining. Mild winters allow local deer populations to explode, but bitter winters can result in mass starvation.

Deer will eat most plants, but their favorites include sugar maple seedlings, fruits, grasses, farm crops, and small succulents. Deer look most impressive in autumn: full of vigor and fattened from plentiful food, the mating season begins. Bucks can top 200 pounds. Antlers, though made of bone, can grow up an inch per day. In autumn they mature and the ceremonial sparring to determine mating rights begins. The antlers drop in early winter and then mice, shrews, and other small animals quickly devour them for their calcium.

Mothers bear young in May and June. Within a few hours, fawns are on their feet. Since running is a deer's primary defense, fawns must quickly master this skill. Mature deer can run at speeds in excess of 40 miles per hour. The fawns lose their spots by autumn. Less than 50% of deer reach adulthood, but those adults can live up to 11 years.

Stinging nettles, an often unwelcome forest resident with their formic acid-filled thorns, dominate large patches of ground. In summer, small white flowers decorate this succulent plant. Jewelweed, its antidote, is harder to find. An ounce of prevention—avoidance—is often the only option. In spring, many other plants decorate the mountainside. Common, Canada, white sweet, and downy yellow violets, purple trillium, foamflower, kidney-leaf buttercups, mitewort, golden alexanders,

Hemlock grove in Mine Hollow.

trout lilies, spring beauties, Dutchman's breeches, dwarf ginkos, wild strawberries, starflowers, jack-in-the-pulpits, and hobblebush all thrive in the moist, lush forests covering Balsam's lower slopes.

"Efficient" best describes the trail. Rising through Rider Hollow at a constant pace, the route parallels the small stream separating Balsam and Haynes Mountains. The path has no rock to climb, nor level sections. The ascent is a steady rise on a moderately steep slope. Regular breaks to inspect the local flora or fauna provide convenient excuses to rest straining muscles.

The hike over Balsam Mountain and a return through Mine Hollow is about five miles. Rider Hollow's parking area sits at 1,900 feet. The trail climbs 1,150 vertical feet through this hollow until meeting the Pine Hill-West Branch Trail. Another 550 feet of ascent brings the north-heading trail to Balsam's summit. Mine Hollow's yellow-blazed trail traces Balsam's northwestern slopes back to Rider Hollow.

Balsam Mountain's summit is true to its name. Balsam fir and its fresh aroma dominate the mountaintop. Grasses, ferns, hobblebush, and other shrubs pepper the open summit. Golden stalks of stiff, dead, and dry grasses fill the landscape beneath a sparse canopy of stunted cherry and yellow birch trees. Near the peak, south of the trail, a small clearing provides a view of Big Indian Mountain.

The summit appears dry compared to surrounding peaks, especially those to the east. Even in these poorly drained soils, the topsoil quickly dries when exposed to the sun. Poor drainage is typical of glaciated areas. The southwestern Catskills, less affected by the continental ice sheets, have fewer poorly drained areas than elsewhere in the range. Alpine glaciers played a large role in the southwestern Catskills, the small, bowl-shaped glaciers gouging steep drainages and new slopes. Balsam's deeply carved northeastern face is a cirque, the result of an alpine glacier that formed on its steep, shaded slopes. As the ice built, its mass and gravity overcame friction, and it began to flow. The ice scours a bowl and its path becomes a steep, U-shaped valley. When the climate warmed, the ice melted leaving the altered landscape. Other Catskill Mountains with distinctive cirques include Mount Tremper and Panther Mountain.

Looking northwest from Balsam Mountain–Hunter and Westkill Mountains.

When the continental ice sheets plowed into the southwestern Catskills, they removed soil and altered drainage patterns. Balsam's summit remained tied to the Catskills' drainage system, unlike the northern Catskills, where the ice sheets endured a few thousand years longer. Although the continental ice sheet eventually overran the area's alpine glaciers, alpine formations returned after the Wisconsin Ice Sheet's greatest advance began to ebb.

Near the summit, above the cirque, an easterly view cuts through the vegetation. The rocky outcrop is a good platform for lunch and reflection. While not a panoramic vista, the dense flora provides a pleasant picture frame for the drifting ridges. Far to the east, Overlook Mountain lifts from the Catskills' eastern edge, its steep southwestern slope introducing the Devil's Path. This long east-west ridge crosses Indian Head, Twin, Sugarloaf, and Plateau Mountains. Olderbark's long summit flows south from Plateau. The western band of the Devil's Path, 4,040-foot Hunter and 3,880-foot Westkill Mountains, sprouts west of Stony Clove, lying due north of Balsam Mountain. Westkill leads into the lower peaks of Northdome and Sherill Mountains. Across from Balsam's northern slopes rises Halcott Mountain, its eastern face thrusting from Lost Clove. In the deep valley below this perch, Route 28 and the Esopus Creek circle Panther Mountain.

On Balsam's northern face, at an elevation of 3,200 feet, an open west-peering overhang spies Dry Brook Ridge and Belleayre Mountain. The scene wraps northward where neighboring Belleayre's gentle mass dominates the scene.

The trail then plunges in to Mine Hollow. Tree size and shape improve as elevation drops. The isolated, sheltered hollow supports a lush forest, and within this deep wilderness are groves of virgin forest. The most impressive is an ancient hemlock grove nestled along the small, steep stream. Heavy shadows and a thick needle carpet, spread from the dark foliage, muffle sound and light. Long ago, large sections of the Catskills wore the soft shadows of hemlock groves, but people's demand for tanbark exchanged the forest's attire for leather bags, shoes, and clothes. Mine Hollow's small grove represents an insignificant percentage, yet still impressive portion, of the forest once dominating the Catskill Mountains.

Winter puts different clothes on Balsam Mountain—white dominates everything. Enhanced by winter's harsh sunlight, snow and ice sparkle like diamonds. Bereft of summer's rich greens and dense foliage, tree buttresses appear to uphold the sky. Cool streams become icy straits as they freeze in their quest to join larger streams, and most will not resume their journey until spring. Only the evergreens show signs of life, their dark green needles in strong contrast with winter's whites, browns, and grays. Wildlife, although more active in summer, leave distinctive signs in winter's cold floors. Animal tracks abound in the snow. Deer signs crisscross the marked trail. Mice too, leave a record of passage. People's footprints lead west and return to the Rider Hollow parking area.

Ice and snow can quickly accumulate near the mountaintop, and thick snows often bury the higher elevations. Trapped clouds lacquer exposed surfaces with hoarfrost, and when lit by the winter sun, the ice turns to molten silver. Seen from the surrounding valleys, the mountains appear like white fire. Landscapes ablaze with winter's icy glory provide few hints that warm summer days will ever grace these frozen, sterile slopes. After experiencing this white wonderland, the joy associated with this wintry ascent is clear.

Balsam Mountain makes a great hike any time of the year. It has numerous attractions on its lower slopes and summit, including diverse foliage, a scenic mountaintop view, bountiful wildlife, and a virgin hemlock stand. The seasonal march provides different scenes throughout the year, whether it is winter's white, summer's greens, or autumn's golds. Balsam's natural references are among the Catskills' best, making this peak highly recommended.

HAYNES AND EAGLE

Hike: Haynes and Eagle Mountains
Roundtrip Hiking Distance: 10.6 miles
County and Town: Ulster, Shandaken and Hardenburgh
Parking: At the end of Rider Hollow Road (accessible via Ulster County Route 49A).
Difficulty: difficult
Bushwhack: no
Elevation Gain: 1420 feet to Haynes, plus 350 more to Eagle

Mile 0.0: Trail starts along Rider Hollow Road (red markers).
0.3: Pass lean-to.
1.6: Reach notch and junction with Pine Hill-West Branch Trail (blue markers). Turn south.
2.5: Summit of Haynes Mountain. Continue south.
4.0: Summit of Eagle Mountain.
5.3: Junction with Seager-Big Indian Trail. Return via route taken.
10.6: Return to Rider Hollow Road.

The Pine Hill-West Branch Trail runs west of Slide Mountain, parallel to Giant Ledge and Panther Mountain. Separated by the Esopus Creek's deep, U-shaped valley, this ridge is the central Catskills' heart. Belleayre and Balsam Mountains mark the trail's northern end, while Big Indian is its southern flank. In the middle of this ridge, the trail crosses the rounded summits of Haynes and Eagle Mountains. The shortest approaches to Eagle Mountain include crossing Haynes. Few open vistas decorate the ridgeline and neither Eagle nor Haynes has any exposed ledges. Instead, they display the Catskills' unique high-

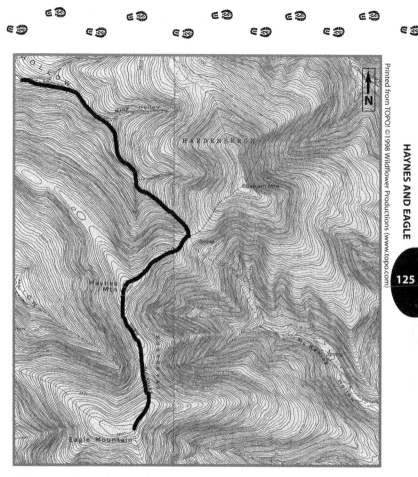

elevation ecosystem. When explored during leafless seasons, skeletal glimpses of the surrounding mountains enhance the forest backgrounds. In late fall, the last splashes of color cling to the mountaintops while the valleys explode with autumn splendor. That season's fleeting scenery makes it a great time to explore these unheralded peaks.

Of the two mountains, only Eagle's 3,600-foot summit qualifies for the Catskill's prominent list of 3,500-foot mountains. Haynes levels off at 3,420 feet, and appears dwarfed by its 3,600-foot neighbors. None of the summits along Pine Hill-West Branch Trail look impressive, but this high, isolated ridge holds one of the Catskills' largest wilderness areas.

Late fall presents extra obstacles, along with the extraordinary seasonal beauty. One relates to traction, the other to orienteering. Leaves once boasting autumn's golds, reds, and oranges now carpet the forest floor in ripening browns. The golden ground easily outshines a cloudy sky. Unfortunately, this is not the only optical deception. The discourteous fallen leaves hide the trail's dirt ribbon, leaving only colored plastic markers for guidance. A crunchy rush emanates with each step through the crisp leaves. Humans rarely surprise animals under these conditions.

Poor traction, another obstacle created by the fallen leaves, makes each step a battle against slipping. Wet conditions magnify the problem. Rocks easily avoided along leaf-free trails lurk beneath autumn's blanket. All this natural engineering requires extra effort to follow the trail and maintain sure footing, but the visual bonuses outweigh the seasonal challenges.

Eagle Mountain's higher elevations harbor a boreal forest in addition to the northern hardwoods on Haynes. When approaching from the north, the shortest trail to Haynes and Eagle begins in Rider Hollow (for a description, see Balsam Mountain). Once above the steep hollow, the path levels before meeting the Pine Hill-West Branch Trail. Haynes, Eagle, and Big Indian Mountains lie to the south. The trail follows a moderate slope as it climbs the main ridge.

Once free of Rider Hollow's steep slopes and straining muscles, the forest's character attracts more attention. Haynes' northern slopes have a typical Catskill forest: a mix of beech, sugar maple, yellow birch, and black cherry. Sugar maple becomes less common as elevation increases. Understory foliage, mainly blackberries, ferns, ground spruce, and grasses, forms a thick tangle above the ground. Wood sorrel's heart-shaped leaves carpet much of the forest floor.

Balsam Mountain's 3,600-foot peak rises north of the trail. Graham and Balsam Lake Mountains define the western horizon. Slide Mountain is east of the trail, its peak thrust above its neighbors and its northern slopes grading into Giant Ledge and Panther Mountain. Tucked behind Slide's southern slopes are Table, Lone, Rocky, and Balsam Cap Mountains. Wittenberg and Cornell rise from behind Giant Ledge as elevation increases.

The climb to Haynes Mountain is a classic Catskill stair-step climb. Horizontal rock strata couple with a veneer of glacial till to create this mountain architecture. The summit builds as a series of steps and level platforms. Short, steep inclines grade into the next level. The peak is not distinct, merely the last platform. The topography reverses on Haynes' southern face.

Tree height decreases as elevation increases. Where the hollows merge into the main ridge, tree tops reach 50 feet. Near Haynes' summit, cooler, windier conditions, and poorer soils limit growth. A woven ceiling of leaves, twigs, and branches rises only 25 feet from the forest floor. Forest characteristics change on Haynes' summit, but it remains dominated by hardwoods. Beech, yellow birch, and black cherry shade most of the peak. Mountain-ash's bright red berries enhance late fall

A winter scene along the Pine Hill-West Branch Trail.

color. Sugar maple cannot grow in these harsh conditions. Stunted trees are common, and few grow more than 30 feet tall. A thick understory of striped maple and hobblebush fills the canopy gaps, and ground vegetation is a collection of wood sorrel, ferns, grasses, and ground spruce. Northern red oak, more typical of dry, exposed slopes at lower elevations, are unexpected members of the surrounding forest. Sometimes, despite man's need to classify and characterize nature, the natural world reveals how limiting classification systems can be.

Unlike most eastern Catskill peaks above 3,000 feet, few conifers grow on Haynes' summit. Only an occasional balsam fir survives, and few reach 15 feet. Red spruce are rare this far west in the Catskills, and none live on Haynes. Local habitats appear acceptable for spruce growth, but environmental factors such as precipitation or soil depth prevent their survival.

Constant gusts force the branches to collide. The sound of clashing wood echoes through the forest. From above and below, the forest's canopy appears uniform. Nonconformers are more subject to ice buildup and strong winds. Winds twist, dwarf, and break the trees, and dead limbs and broken trunks litter the forest floor. When a tree falls, the new gap permits wind and ice to attack the newly exposed trees, further opening the canopy. Replacement saplings help the forest adjust, but the entire community benefits from a smooth canopy. Here, the biggest and most aggressive individuals create conditions for self-destruction.

Haynes' summit holds a moonscape of rocks. A thin layer of glacial till and broken bedrock replaced soils scoured during the ice age. Relentless freezing and thawing cracked, broke, and released large quantities of rock from Haynes' slopes. Soil formation began with the Wisconsin Ice Sheet's final retreat. Small soil pockets have developed between the rock, mostly composed of organic matter and till.

Deep moss carpets cover the rock, surviving on nutrient levels unable to sustain larger plants. Ferns and trees grow in the thicker soil pockets. Shallow, low-fertility soils produce low tree densities. Large canopy gaps allow sunlight to bathe the understory. Ferns, grasses, and shrubs, including hobblebush and huckleberries, thrive in the plentiful sunlight.

After crossing Haynes, the trail continues to Eagle. Once off the exposed summit, the forest becomes taller and healthier. The surrounding vegetation quickly hides Eagle from view. After a short decline, the trail levels off in a small notch and moves onto Eagle Mountain. The climb begins at a moderate slope. Haynes' mass hovers north of the trail. Beech, birch, black cherry, and striped maple dominate the forest, and few understory trees grow in the thick shade. In the notch, deeper tills and soil cover the bedrock, but both thin as elevation increases. Another stair-step climb accompanies the upward journey. Mosses coat the sun-shielded, north-facing rocky surfaces. In the northern sky, Balsam Mountain's summit now dwarfs Haynes.

By the time the path reaches 3,500-feet, balsam fir enters the forest. Large tangles of hobblebush frame the understory, complemented by ferns, wood sorrel, and dark, wet mosses. Once on the summit shelf, a subtle incline traces the route to Eagle's peak. The gently sloping mountaintop holds an isolated environment found on Eagle and neighboring high peaks. Each is an island of boreal habitat among a sea of temperate forests.

A final lift introduces a healthy forest of balsam fir, yellow birch, and mountain-ash, and eliminates the last forest similarities between Eagle and Haynes. The 180 feet that thrust Eagle above Haynes produce an environment not found on the lower summit. A subalpine, balsam fir forest develops, but yellow birch also thrive in the cool, damp conditions. Late fall mixes the fir's dark green needles, yellow birch's pale golden-yellow leaves, and mountain-ash's bright red berries with the rusty-orange of dried ferns.

Thick vegetation encloses Eagle's upper elevations, focusing interest on the immediate area. A sturdy collection of Devonian sandstones and conglomerates uphold Eagle's highest slopes. The conglomerate, Catskill puddingstone, tops many Catskill summits. Rounded quartz pebbles, freed from this sandy matrix, line the trail. Crusty lichens thrive on the exposed rock outcrops, shading them tan, gray, and green. Rock tripe, an edible species resembling a brown potato chip, grows in large colonies.

After crossing the level summit, the trail descends Eagle's southern face. The stair-step topography returns. Big Indian looms to the south, and the trail heads toward its massive form. Doubletop Mountain's twin mounds rise beyond Big Indian. Along Doubletop's top ridge are a mature stand of fir trees, visible only to the eagle-eyed. Like the descent from Haynes, the trees on Eagle's southern slope quickly increase in size. Warmer temperatures, sheltered slopes, and thicker soils foster the change. Hobblebush dominates large patches along the trail. Coarse, dark blackberry leaves linger late into autumn. Drying ferns continue to paint the landscape orange-brown.

The path moves from the ridge's center to its eastern side while descending the Eagle's southern face. Panther Mountain, Giant Ledge, and Slide Mountain fill the forest gaps east of the trail. Glimpses north reveal other Catskill profiles, including Northdome, Westkill, Hunter, and Plateau Mountains.

The deep notch separating Eagle and Big Indian Mountains provides a milder environment and allows the forest to thrive. Red maple, sugar maple, and hemlock join black cherry, yellow birch, and beech. The path then returns to the ridge's center and meets the trail traversing Shandaken Hollow and Dry Brook Valley. The Pine Hill-West Branch Trail continues toward Big Indian Mountain. The return trip entails backtracking, bushwhacking, or a long walk down Shandaken Hollow and along Dry Brook.

Despite their limited views, Haynes and Eagle make for pleasant hiking. Constant yet subtle changes and forest gradations escort the path. Local topography generates picturesque scenes on a small scale often missed when searching for wide vistas. Season also plays a role, refining the landscape on a daily basis. Scenes encountered one time of the year yield to changes in color, texture, and setting come the next season. Variety abounds, making Haynes and Eagle Mountains worth visiting any time of year.

BIG INDIAN

Hike: Big Indian Mountain
Roundtrip Hiking Distance: 10.0 miles
County and Town: Ulster, Shandaken and Hardenburgh
Parking: At the end of Dry Brook Road (Ulster County Route 49).
Difficulty: difficult
Bushwhack: no
Elevation Gain: 1700 feet

Mile: 0.0: Begin Seager-Big Indian Mountain Trail (yellow markers) off Dry Brook Road.
1.3: Cross Dry Brook Stream, enter Shandaken Hollow.
2.1: Pass Shandaken Brook lean-to.
3.0: Trail ends at Pine Hill-West Branch Trail (blue markers). Turn south.
4.8: Trail's crest on Big Indian. Bushwhack east to summit.
5.0: Reach Big Indian's summit. Return via same route.
10.0: Return to Seager-Big Indian Mountain trailhead.

Local legend tells the story of Winnisook, an eight-foot tall Indian who roamed the Catskill Mountains in search of game. He loved a beautiful white girl who lived on a farm in the Esopus Valley. The girl loved Winnisook too, but when her father discovered the affair, he forbade it. The couple ran away. When the father learned of the elopement, he gathered his neighbors and chased the Indian brave. Some endings tell of Winnisook's death at the hands of his pursuers. Others tell of his valiant sacrifice to save his love. Whatever the ending, Winnisook did not leave this world untouched. His body became a mountain. This mountain, Winnisook's final resting place, is Big Indian.

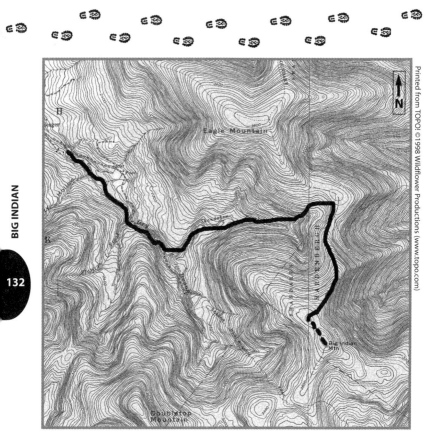

Big Indian rises west of Slide Mountain. At 3,700 feet, it is the Catskills' 16th highest peak. Loftier summits surround Big Indian, so its stature is often lost in the shadows of neighboring peaks. Its inconspicuous shape, a generic-looking mound along the Phoenicia-East Branch Trail, further reduces its notoriety. Big Indian's unremarkable shape often appears engulfed within a higher peak. To the east, Slide Mountain, king of the Catskills, rises 480 feet higher than Big Indian. Showy Doubletop, 160 feet taller than Big Indian, forms a western backdrop. Farther west, Graham Mountain does the same. To the north is Eagle Mountain, 100 feet lower than Big Indian, but its similar shape further obscures Big Indian's identity.

Many Catskill overlooks include Big Indian among its sights, but few highlight it as an important peak. Despite this lack of prominence, Big Indian is a rewarding destination. Its slopes offer unique habitats and geography, and hold many adventures. To those with spirit, Big Indian's true summit is an easy bushwhack from the trail. The actual peak is nestled within a mature balsam fir forest, bypassed by engineered footpaths.

The most direct marked trail to Big Indian begins at the Seager parking area along Dry Brook. The trail follows this lively stream until it climbs Shandaken Hollow and leads into the notch separating Eagle and Big Indian Mountains. At its lower terminus, the trail is a public easement, paralleling Dry Brook's western bank. The active stream often floods its banks and the path. Small tributaries slice the path as they complete their vigorous journey into Dry Brook. Wet ground and a twisting route can make for a difficult trip. Finding and following the trail can become frustrating.

Cut in the mid-1900s, the valley's young forest consists mostly of thin trees. Large rotting stumps stud the rocky ground and release nutrients for the next generation. The stumps stand as monuments to a grander forest cut to feed paper mills and construction. Cohorts of yellow birch saplings, shrubs, and grasses line Dry Brook's floodplain. Floods drown trees, producing and maintaining the open environment. Many short-lived plants thrive after periods of high water.

Beech, yellow birch, red maple, and sugar maple dominate the local forest. Shaded by a dense canopy, understory growth is minimal, but discharged leaves and fallen wood cover the forest floor. Hearty colonies of ferns and grasses sprout wherever sunlight reaches the ground. By the mid-1900s, lumber companies had harvested most of the area's large trees. Only hemlocks, cut in large numbers for tanbark in the mid-1800s, but not desired since 1900, remained standing. A few mature, drooping hemlocks mix with scores of younger hardwoods. In a few places, the hemlocks form small groves. Blanketed in cool shade, the groves radiate peace, isolation, and comfort. Nestled between the hemlocks and mountain stream, the trail passes through cooler, moister, and dimmer environments.

Dry Brook has an underfit valley, much larger than the stream's volume indicates. The U-shaped valley developed during the ice age. Present until 11,000 years ago, glaciers scoured, enlarged, and rounded the Catskills' valleys. The ice has long since retreated, but erosion continues as water and wind degrade and transport the Catskills grain by grain.

The stream is not the only active purveyor of erosion. Steep slopes, many without supportive vegetation, lose soils and rock to gravity. A few trees linger at the slope's precipice. They struggle to maintain their upright position, yet many lie in ruin far below their onetime neighbors. The unstable slopes will remain in flux until erosion smooths the hillsides or only exposed rock remains.

Fish, mainly trout, swim in the clear, placid pools. Most live among the calm stretches; however, a few choose more active sites and avoid competition. As they feed on aquatic and flying insects, the fish fatten in the healthy stream environment. Trout have excellent eyesight. They quickly dart to safety among the rocky streambottom when humans or other potential predators move along the shore. Crayfish and salamanders also live among the rocks.

Where resistant bedrock intersects the streamcourse, the valley constricts to a narrow channel. Previously calm water smashes into stubborn rock formations, roaring to life as clear water turns white. Many of these whitewater stretches evolve into small waterfalls or sharp cascades. As the streambed climbs, such spots become more common.

As the valley climbs, it changes. Now V-shaped, the stream reveals its 11,000 years of erosional prowess along the valley floor. The higher walls retain their glacially inspired U-shape. With sight and hearing distracted by the stream's power and beauty, working muscles take little notice of the steeper slopes

Fixed to the west bank until parting from Dry Brook Valley, the trail then ascends Shandaken Hollow. Dry Brook continues south, but the trail crosses the brisk water at a wide ford. In low water, a few rocks can offer a safe, dry passage, but except in dry seasons, crossing Dry Brook without getting wet is difficult. Once across the stream, the path rises quickly. Still more dirt road than trail, the wide tracks provide an easy route. Shandaken Brook drains the hollow and escorts the trail until both terminate in the notch separating Eagle and Big Indian Mountains. Lively and noisy, the clear, cold water makes its presence known. The trail has no choice but to follow. Doubletop Mountain's twin peaks loom through the hollow's western opening.

Hemlocks clothe the streambank in mottled patches of muted green, soft browns, and heavy shadow. A northern hardwood forest coats the slopes beyond the hemlocks. Relatively undisturbed, the forest canopy lifts 60 feet above the ground. A mix of saplings and shrubs compose the sun-flecked understory. Stinging nettles grow with ruthless abandon along the trail.

Short, steep inclines blend with long gradual ascents along the hollow's lower reaches. Near the hollow's midpoint, a gentler topography prevails. Shandaken Brook hugs the hollow's southern wall, while tall forests grace the drier slopes. The forest is older and more vigorous than in Dry Brook Valley, protected by high ridges and nourished on

Shandaken Hollow.

subdued slopes. Tall black cherry trees tower above the landscape. Commerce values these trees in the thousands of dollars, but to the forest community they are priceless. They produce food and shelter for wildlife, store water, nutrients and energy, and prevent soil erosion. Also common are large sugar maples and beech. Hemlocks reach large dimensions in the sheltered cove. An occasional paper birch, its bark graying in old age, stands out among the other trunks. White ash and red maple complete the forest stand. A thick understory creates a second level of green. Within the canopy's shade thrives a host of sugar maple saplings, other small trees, shrubs, and herbaceous vegetation. Stinging nettles are among the most prolific. Thick patches of the thorny plant line the path and discourage wandering. In fall, when most leaves pave the forest floor, the nettles stubbornly hold theirs. The leaves shrivel and die on their stems, leaving stands of brittle, useless nettle leaves to greet the approaching winter. On a windy day the eerie sound of shaking leaves rattles the forest, a sound most appropriate around Halloween.

Red and gray rocks share the ground with soil, moss, and small plants. The red stone takes its color from iron-oxide. The rusty hues attest to an oxygen-rich environment at the time of deposition. Since the Catskills' sediments accumulated among river deltas, oxygen was available. Most rocks containing iron within the Catskills are red. Gray rocks usually have little iron. Green rocks result when iron occurs in reduced form. Reduced iron forms in oxygen-free conditions as found in marine environments. Green strata are more common west of the Catskills' highest peaks.

A Catskill forest with such large trees is rare in the late twentieth century. Wide tracts of mature forest once covered the Catskills, but loggers then harvested the mountain slopes. Despite the area's high-quality forests, it is far from pristine. Cut stumps occasionally mar the mountainside. The similar-sized, even-aged trees are another sign of past disturbance. True virgin growth typically has more variation in size and age. Also virgin forests cut in the 1800s had more mature hemlocks than found in current stands. The few remaining large hemlocks are impressive sights, but imagine Shandaken Hollow filled with dark hemlocks, each tree almost twice as high and wide as the largest currently here.

The forest maintains its large, healthy character as the trail heads for steeper slopes. The stream and its small valley move south. The mountain continually offers steeper terrain, and the trail must follow. Traction is less sure on the angled, rocky ground. Pieces of mountain slide down the trail as feet knock them free from unstable resting places. Breath becomes short, hearts race, and progress slows. As fatigue increases, the large trees along the trail become more interesting. A stop to investigate appeals more with each step. Tired muscles and curious minds both benefit from the rest, but regardless of the reasons for the frequent stops, the notch remains fixed atop the hollow. Eventually, even the most curious explorers must proceed.

The long climb ends abruptly at the notch separating Eagle and Big Indian Mountains. With the notch comes a new perspective of the local geography. Big Indian's massive slopes surround the hollow to the south, east, and west. The summit remains a distant goal, but it is no longer the remote peak seen from nearby valleys. Eagle Mountain stands to the north, its summit hidden by closer ridgelines. A small cliff stands at the head of Shandaken Hollow. From it, Graham Mountain makes one last appearance before fading among Big Indian's forested slopes.

A turn south toward Big Indian marks the end of Shandaken Hollow. The trail's rise is gentle, sticking to a ridge. The notch's forest composition remains similar to the slopes below, but the trees are smaller. As the trail climbs Big Indian, the forest quickly loses additional stature. Hemlock and sugar maple are the first to disappear. Beyond the forest are Fir and Slide Mountains. Slide's 4,180 feet rise well above any other peak.

The trail then traces a stair-step pattern typical of the Catskills. The sky moves closer and winds increase with each step. Mountain maple, mountain-ash, beech, black cherry, and yellow birch anchor a forest typical of the western Catskills' upper elevations. Twisted, dwarfed, and battered, the trees huddle together for protection against the elements. The thinning tree cover allows glimpses north to Eagle,

Haynes, Balsam, and Belleayre Mountains. To the west are Balsam Lake Mountain and Dry Brook Ridge.

The sandstones upholding Big Indian's summit slowly build to a crescendo. Dense vegetation competes with rocky terrain for mountaintop dominance. Tons of loose stone outcrops pepper the summit. Mosses and lichens side with the rocks, liberally growing on the gray sandstones and multi-hued conglomerates. Where the soil is thick enough, dense stands of balsam fir and mountain-ash clothe the mountaintop. The firs' intense foliage, along with mountain-ashes' bright red berries, create a Christmas-like atmosphere. Branches reaching for the sun form tunnels over the trail. The thin soils limit forest cover, but the open canopy allows abundant sunlight to reach the ground. With the light and tree-provided windbreaks, the understory of hobblebush, ferns, and grasses thrives.

The trail caps a small rise and then descends Big Indian's southern face; however, this crest is not Big Indian's summit. A balsam fir stand to the east catches the eye. The rise they inhabit appears higher than the cresting trail. Topographic maps confirm this perception. Big Indian's summit is 3,700 feet above sea level, but the path barely reaches 3,600 feet. The trail ignores this challenge, abandoning the adventure for points below. To find Big Indian's true summit requires a bushwhack.

Big Indian's true summit lies a quarter-mile east of the path. Two gentle ascents lie between the trail and the peak. It is an easy trek to the elevational island. Astute observation reveals a meandering trail through the vegetation, but tracing the highest ridge also leads to the summit. Along the route, a partial view reveals Doubletop's twin peaks. West of Doubletop is Graham. A thick, healthy stand of mature balsam fir cap the first rise. After a small dip, a 50-foot climb culminates the short journey. The bright orange registration box marks Big Indian's final thrust into the sky. From this colorful monolith, an unmarked trail leads toward the notch between Big Indian and Fir Mountains.

In contrast with the stands of balsam fir on neighboring ridges, hardwoods dominate Big Indian's summit. Black cherry, beech, and yellow birch compose most of the forest. Hobblebush, a tangled plant often true to its name, share the understory with beech saplings. Fir trees, especially young ones, are rare. If the species is to survive on Big Indian, it must reproduce successfully, and at the moment this is not happening. The lack of reproduction is a mystery. Increasing average temperatures favor deciduous species over fir, and air quality may play a possible, yet unproven, role. Even in this golden age of science, many of nature's secrets remain hidden.

Big Indian's summit offers no views. Beyond its elevational distinction, it is an unremarkable place. After returning to the marked trail, the path continues south along Biscuit Brook's headwaters. The landscape retains its upland character of rock and scraggly trees. One actively fights nature's forces, while the other passively sits through the ages. In the end both, will lose, yet the earth will create new entities to replace them.

As the trail winds south and west, it approaches Doubletop Mountain. A high ridge connects the trail with this higher neighbor. A line of blazed trees, marking the boundary of state land, crosses the main trail. The small path heads west toward Doubletop. The isolated ridge holds spectacular scenery and adventure.

Big Indian Mountain is one of the Catskills' least known, and thus, least impacted mountains. It offers no open vistas, relying on challenge and adventure to bring people to its slopes. With its legends, adventure, and unspoiled wilderness, Big Indian needs little else to recommend it.

FIR MOUNTAIN

Fir Mountain rises to the east-southeast of Big Indian Mountain on the upper Esopus Valley's western slopes. A healthy forest of balsam fir and a set of struggling hardwoods cap its summit. When Arnold Henry Guyot, the first person to accurately calculate the Catskills' elevations, explored this area in 1879, he misidentified this 3,620-foot peak, then called Spruce Mountain. Fir was its lower, southeastern neighbor. History perpetuated this error.

Fir's summit rises along a ridgeline spreading southeast from Big Indian Mountain. A series of sporadic deer trails leads through a forest of tangled hobblebush, yellow birch, and thick evergreens. An off-trail route via the Biscuit Brook lean-to provides a more direct approach. Dense vegetation encloses Fir's summit, and heavy shadows cloak the mountaintop. No vistas open from the peak, but an exposed sandstone ledge a quarter-mile northwest reveals a fine view. It is easy to spot Fir Mountain, as its distinctive profile is visible from where New York Route 28 crosses Birch Creek.

THE SOUTHERN CATSKILLS:
PEEKAMOOSE AND TABLE

Hike: Peekamoose and Table Mountains
One-way Hiking Distance: 8.2 miles
County and Town: Ulster, Denning
Parking: At the end of Denning Road (accessible by Sullivan
    County Route 19 in Claryville) and along Peekamoose Road
    (Ulster County Route 42), 10 miles south of State Route 28A
    and 6.4 miles north of State Route 55A.
Difficulty: difficult
Bushwhack: no
Elevation Gain: to Table—1600 feet; down from Peekamoose to
    trailhead—2650 feet

(one-way hike, requires two vehicles)
Mile: 0.0: Parking area at terminus of Denning Road (yellow
    markers).
    1.1: Junction with Peekamoose-Table Trail. Turn east (right,
    blue markers).
    1.4: Denning lean-to.
    3.9: Summit of Table.
    4.6: Notch between Table and Cornell.
    4.9: Summit of Peekamoose. Begin descent.
    5.6: Pass old trail on left.
    8.2: Reach parking area along Peekamoose Road.

Two small tributaries drain Slide Mountain's southern slopes. As these waters leave the Catskills' highest lands, they gather to form Rondout Creek and the East Branch of the Neversink River. Once away from Slide, these two streams diverge: one flowing west, the other

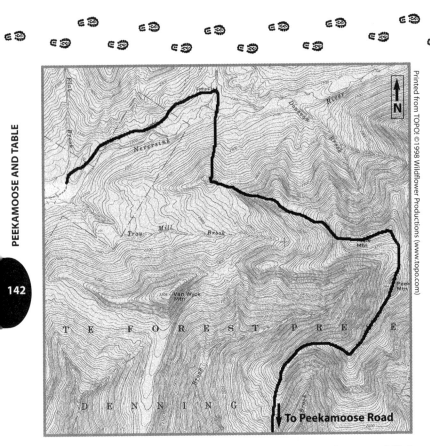

To Peekamoose Road

south. The high ground between them holds the southern Catskills' highest peaks, Peekamoose and Table Mountains.

Both mountains reach among the Catskills' highest summits. Table lifts 3,847 feet above sea level, and Peekamoose is four feet its junior. White conglomerates, a sign of their common geology, cover their upper elevations. Only Slide and Cornell Mountains hold more of this resistant rock. Peekamoose and Table also have similar forest communities. The only exception is Peekamoose's lowest slopes along Rondout Creek.

Regardless of similarities and differences, proximity binds these two mountains. Easily hiked together, Peekamoose and Table make a good circuit if two vehicles are available. Roads from Denning, a small town along the East Branch of the Neversink River, provide the best access to Table Mountain. The trail begins where the paved road ends. The river, actually a lively mountain stream, inhabits an underfit valley carved by glaciers and meltwater about 12,000 years ago. The trail, an old logging road, rises along the river's western bank. The surrounding forest is a mix of hemlock, beech, and yellow birch. Thin soil, composed largely of humus and till, color the earth black.

Sheltered between high mountains, these forests escape the strongest winds. Trees grow straight and tall, unaffected by the storms that devastate the higher elevations. Despite the calmer atmosphere, downed trees litter the landscape, their uplifted root systems confirming the unsupportive, shallow soils.

The trail remains level as it follows the stream. Forest composition mixes hemlock and yellow birch into stands of light, dark, and peeling bark. Sugar maple dominates the understory. In early spring, violets, trout lilies, spring beauties, and purple trillium poke into the sun-dappled understory.

Then the trail splits. The northern fork winds toward Slide Mountain, while the eastern fork gently descends into a swampy area. A bottomland forest fills this marsh, its water feeding the Neversink River. Extensive root systems supply support in the soft soils. Mosses blanket the land in green, covering gray rocks and brown tree bark.

After the wetland, the trail rises onto drier ground and a forest of sugar maple, beech, and yellow birch—the Catskills' most common forest cover. Striped maple is common in the understory. The trail then descends to the East Branch of the Neversink River, its braided river channels crisscrossing the valley. Normally, water fills only a few channels. Trees sparsely populate the flood plain, discouraged by periodic flooding. High waters deprive roots of oxygen and drown them, and without functioning roots, the tree dies. The frequent flooding also hindered man's attempts to live here. A few large trees survived the floods and monopolize the open floodplain.

The Denning lean-to sits on the river's eastern bank. Situated like a cozy mountain retreat, the shelter is a comfortable residence among the untamed forest. Curbs of neatly placed stones line the trail as it follows the riverbank. After passing the lean-to, the trail begins its assault on Table Mountain.

The steep climb up Table's western flank keeps a continuous grade. Elevation increases quickly. Wildcat Mountain stands behind the trail, its 3,100-foot peak a benchmark for elevation estimates. The strenuous slopes make for slow progress. A northern hardwood forest still blankets the land, but tree cover thins on the inhospitable ground. Mature striped maple, 45 feet tall, share the canopy. Remnants of the last ice age, periglacial boulders and loose rock, line and cross the path.

After a long, climbing trek, the path reaches a 2,800-foot peak. Table's two highest neighbors loom through the forest's wooden skeleton: Slide Mountain to the north, and Peekamoose to the southwest. Table's remaining elevation towers in the foreground. Once over the knob, the trail descends into a small notch. The drop feels like betrayal by the land. A tall forest grows in the protected depression.

Not a popular trail, the small dirt ribbon weaves its way up Table's western slopes. Small, spring-fed streams cross the route and nourish the lush forests. Springs and underground drainages appear, soak a few feet of ground, and disappear. Since each 1,000-foot elevation gain is the equivalent of moving 250 miles north, these slopes have a climate akin to valleys 500 miles to the north. As the elevation climbs, winds increase, and tree height decreases. Branches crash in pulses of wooden thunder. The result is a collection of dwarfed, malformed birch and cherry forest. Healthy, picture-perfect balsam fir mix into this wind-whipped upper hardwood forest. Next to the well-proportioned evergreens, the local hardwoods form twisted and dwarfed wooden sculptures.

The trail winds onto Table's southwestern face. Although these slopes receive 65 inches of annual precipitation, the sun's direct rays warm and dry the land, producing a mesic habitat. When compared to other Catskill slopes at the same elevation, the vegetation and forest structure differ in this drier environment. Species adjusted to dry soils thrive, and some plants common at lower, warmer elevations persist on these slopes. Vegetation and leaf litter are dry and crispy. Decay rates and fire frequency are high. As a result, grasses and blueberries capitalize on the sunny, open spaces.

A subalpine forest of balsam fir and yellow birch dominates Table's windswept upper elevations. A tangle of dry, golden grasses carpet the ground. The rocky path skirts Table's profile before climbing onto its backbone. Small northward views open where tree cover thins. In one clearing, the parting vegetation and steep slopes combine to produce an expansive vista. When backlit, a deep blue sky and fluffy white clouds often enhance this scene. Slide Mountain towers north of the overlook, its lofty status apparent among its Catskill brethren. A series of saddles and sharp ridges connect Slide with Cornell and Friday Mountains. Doubletop's split top dominates the western sky, claiming Big Indian within its silhouette. North of Big Indian, a ridge leads to Eagle and Fir Mountains.

Looking north at Slide Mountain from Table's summit.

Crushed white and light gray quartz pebbles pave the final approach to Table's summit. Similar to Slide's upper elevations, the stone spreads like a tame garden pathway through the wilderness. The rock is rare, capping only the southern Catskill high peaks. Derived from Catskill conglomerate, these resistant quartz pebbles once were part of the Acadian Mountains. After eroding from the waning mountains, rivers transported these sediments west and deposited the heavy, sandy particles and larger, rounded quartz stones among sluggish river deltas.

Table's summit profile is a flat-topped surface that provides the mountain's name. Although hard to detect, the true summit lies at the ridge's western end. After reaching this crest, the trail slowly dips eastward. Balsam fir and the occasional yellow birch cover the entire area. A stiff breeze is common, and gusty winds frequently buffet the mountaintop. Abused by the elements, the trees grow low and dense.

Slightly north of the trail, as it approaches Table's eastern end, a north-facing vista opens. The scene unveils as a 120-degree panorama to north and west. Tough roots ensconce a sparse stand of hearty balsam fir and yellow birch. The nearby trees add depth to the scene. Grasses, green and thriving in spring, golden and dry by early summer, fill the open spaces. Among the distant landscape, Slide Mountain monopolizes the northern skyline. An east-flowing ridge spans the gap to Cornell Mountain. Behind this knife-edged ridge rise Hunter and Westkill Mountains. At 4,040 feet, Hunter is the Catskills' second highest peak. Sharp-peaked Westkill is the sixth highest. To the west are another set of high mountains including Doubletop and Graham, the mightiest peaks in the western Catskills. The mountains lining the upper Esopus Valley—Hemlock, Spruce, Fir, Big Indian, Eagle, Hayes, Balsam, and twin-lobed Belleayre—lie north of these giants.

Once beyond the viewpoint, Table's topography dives. A trailless ridge drifts to the northeast, rising again as Lone Mountain, often visible through the trees. The trail sharply descends southeast, into a notch. The path's descent eases as it threads a forest of yellow birch and balsam fir. Hobblebush and dried grasses crowd the dirt path. Yellow trout lilies and purple and white spring beauties announce spring's arrival. Above the notch stands Peekamoose's aggressive summit. Now situated to the rear, Table's distinctive features fade into memories.

A broad notch, never falling below 3,500 feet, separates the two mountains. A thick spruce-fir community holds the secluded pass. Twenty-foot conifers weave dense thickets on either side of the path to create an impenetrable barrier. Starved for light, lower branches wither and die. A graveyard of dead sticks fills the shadowy space beneath the dark green canopy. Glaciation scoured this slope into a layer of flat, poorly drained sandstone. Wet soils result. Composed mainly of decaying organic matter, a black mud full of acidic humus frosts the notch.

The 325-foot climb up Peekamoose is easy. A small rut, often filled with runoff, charges down the trail. Table rises north of the path, a single orientation beacon among a tree-choked sky. A spruce-fir forest covers Peekamoose's summit. Dwarfed by the harsh climate, these trees must survive seven months of ice, wind, and snow. Broken branches, stripped needles, and uprooted trunks litter the ground.

A small clearing accompanies the trail onto the summit. Pickets of conifers enclose the sunny opening. A large conglomerate boulder is the center of attention. The huge rock is a collection of milky quartz crystals and scattered colored stones. Born with the Acadian Mountains, these stones are 450 million years old. They were rounded and transported by water erosion, then collected among the sediments forming the Catskill clastic wedge (delta). Uplift occurred during the Appalachian Orogeny. Dropped during the retreat of the Wisconsin Ice Sheet, the glacial erratic memorializes that frozen age. No longer encased in ice, the elements erode exposed surfaces into a rough, sandy coating.

The dense conifer pickets prevent open views; however, the large boulder's boost provides a look at the northern and eastern skyline. Still hampered by the tree cover, these small views, however, provide beauty and orientation. Table Mountain dominates the northwestern skyline. Lone and Rocky Mountains lead toward the Burroughs Range, a few of its peaks barely slipping into view.

After crossing Peekamoose's summit, the trail continues south into the Rondout Valley. Accompanying the descent is a change in forest communities. The spruce-fir forest gives way to open stands of stout yellow birch and black cherry. The broken canopy allows grasses, flowers, and shrubs to grow. In spring, the slope wears bouquets of white, yellow, and pink. Thick clumps of tangled hobblebush, and sturdy striped maple populate the understory. Angled to the south, the sun bathes this slope with heat and light. Since the land's topography parallels the sun's incoming rays, it receives more energy and modifies the microclimate. The concentrated sunlight and fast-draining slopes alter the local habitat and forest community.

Once the land levels again, a spruce-fir forest returns. Without the concentrated sunlight, a subalpine environment again rules the land. The long, level ridgeline heads west. When ascending the trail from the Rondout Valley, this ridge appears as a false summit. A lush spruce-fir forest perpetuates this belief.

After traversing this flat shelf, the path drops onto another level area. Again the forest changes. Northern hardwoods blend with the spruce and fir trees. Blueberry bushes thrive on the open, fire-tempered ground. In dry years, especially during the Catskill's logging era, fire was common to these slopes. High winds and harsh winters ensure that few large trees develop. Disturbances are the rule, not the exception. The trail winds through this weather-abused forest and gently sloping terrain until Peekamoose's false summit rises far to the northeast.

The trail makes a tight westward curve as it exits the ledge. The short switchback and small drops reveal a small cliff and a series of views. Atop the sheer rock ledges, sandstone platforms open into 180 to 270-degree panoramas. Ashokan High Point anchors the vistas' northeastern limits. The Kanape Valley carves High Point's southern slopes. Mombaccus and Little Rocky Mountains compose the next ridge south. The deep, shaded Rondout Valley runs east of the rounded peaks. VanWyck and Wildcat Mountains fill the southwest. Doubletop's twin peaks and Balsam Lake Mountain dominate the northwestern sky. Smaller peaks fade into Sullivan and Delaware Counties. Table's wide, flat 3,847-foot summit ridge fills the northwestern skyline.

After curling onto the viewpoint, the trail returns to a southerly course. A few steps below the overlook an unmarked path heads south. Abandoned, this old trail follows Buttermilk Falls Brook to Rondout Creek. Buttermilk Falls leaps a cliff wall near the trail's lower end.

The maintained route passes steep rock walls and uses switchbacks to keep the descent reasonable. The trail follows Peekamoose Mountain's curving southeastern spur. A scraggly set of upper hardwoods struggle to survive among the rocky soil. Once beyond the rough terrain, the land softens and a northern hardwood forest reclaims the land. Yellow birch, black cherry, beech, and maple compose trailside vegetation. Tree height increases as elevation decreases. Red spruce and balsam fir disappear in the milder conditions.

Another southerly bend takes the trail past a small ledge. A balanced rock hovers above the lichen-encrusted sandstone. Despite minimal support, the balanced boulder's position remains stable. Closer inspection reveals the boulder's composition as different from the ledge. Glaciation created this situation. When the continental ice sheets buried northern North America, they collected rock and debris. Carried as a tourist does souvenirs, the ice transported embedded objects hundreds of miles. When temperatures warmed and the ice melted, these keepsakes became till. Sand, silt, rocks, boulders, and erratics littered the newly exposed ground. In rare cases, the random deposition left boulders balanced on ledges.

While the trail continues down Peekamoose's southern face, the trees continue to grow taller as climate moderates. The trailside woods hold a high canopied forest of northern red oak, bigtooth aspen, black cherry, white ash, shagbark hickory, yellow birch, a few sugar maples, and the occasional beech. The solid canopy rises like a vaulted ceiling supported by flying buttresses. Species composition reflects an early successional community. Some, especially bigtooth aspen, grow only in direct sunlight. Sprouting after early-20th-century logging, these first generation trees date the forest.

Beech saplings populate the dimly lit understory. A local climax species, these beech represent the future canopy dominants. A few sugar maple saplings, another climax species, hover above the forest floor. Most of the ground is free of herbaceous vegetation. Brown leaf litter, the detritus of past years' growth, carpets the forest floor.

As the trail nears its southern terminus along Rondout Creek, a few stands of red pine lift their scaly red-brown trunks into the canopy. Planted in pure stands to help restore logged forests, these trees cannot reproduce without fire. Since the forests and damper conditions returned, fires are uncommon, so the pines will leave the local vegetation. Already, northern hardwoods sprout below them.

The path makes its final descent along an old roadbed. A steep grade returns the path to civilization. The Rondout's energetic waters flavor the air with a turbulent chorus.

Peekamoose and Table Mountains are giants among the Catskills, yet they seem isolated from the range, as if stuffed in a corner. Once found, they make a welcome addition to the Catskill collection. Both peaks feature a rich natural history and quality adventures. Since they alone dominate the southeastern Catskills, their slopes survey a unique perspective.

THE WESTERN CATSKILLS

The western Catskills are a set of high, isolated peaks. They are not as rugged as their eastern neighbors, yet the mountain summits rival the region's loftiest. Second-growth forests coat the area with reclaimed wilderness. The land is harsh, difficult to farm. It has little else to offer beyond scenery, wildlife, and peace. Doubletop, Graham, and Balsam Lake Mountains form a west-trending ridge-line anchored by Big Indian and Slide Mountains. Dry Brook Ridge is the western Catskills' final sentinel, overlooking the numerous hills of Delaware County and beyond.

Slide from Doubletop.

DOUBLETOP MOUNTAIN

Hike: Doubletop Mountain
Roundtrip Hiking Distance: 13.2 miles
County and Town: Ulster, Denning and Hardenburgh
Parking: At the end of Dry Brook Road (Ulster County Route 49).
Difficulty: difficult
Bushwhack: yes, 3.2 miles
Elevation Gain: 1880 feet (plus 440 additional feet due to drops along the bushwhack route)

Mile: 0.0: Begin Seager-Big Indian Mountain Trail (yellow markers) off Dry Brook Road.

1.3: Cross Dry Brook Stream, enter Shandaken Hollow.

2.1: Pass Shandaken Brook lean-to.

3.0: Trail ends at Pine Hill-West Branch Trail (blue markers). Turn south.

4.8: Trail's crest on Big Indian.

5.0: Encounter boundary of state land (poorly marked).

5.8: Cross lowpoint between Big Indian and Doubletop Mountains.

6.4: Doubletop's northern summit.

6.6: Doubletop's southern (true) summit. Trace the route back to Seager Parking Area.

13.2: Return to Seager parking area.

Doubletop Mountain is the highest and most conspicuous peak west of Slide Mountain. Twin, rounded summits compose Doubletop's highest points and provide its name. Easily recognized, it sits between Big Indian and Graham Mountains, and links Graham and Balsam Lake

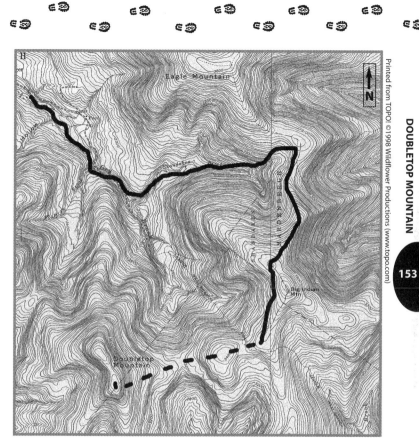

Mountains with the Catskills' main ridges. Tall, dark stands of balsam fir blanket both of Doubletop's summits. At 3,860 feet, Doubletop is the Catskills' eighth-highest peak. A backcountry challenge, it is the Catskills' highest summit without a trail.

Approaches to Doubletop have three common factors: none are easy, all require off-trail exploration, and each is long and tiring. As a trail-less peak, the Catskill 3500 Club maintains a registry, but finding it is a quest reserved for the northern summit.

It is hard to choose a path when hiking Doubletop. While approaches begin from each cardinal direction, the eastern and southern routes are easiest to navigate. The southern approach lifts from Frost Valley, following High Falls Brook. A trail, with no well-defined starting point, surmounts Doubletop's southern shoulder before completing the journey. The only other man-made navigational aid is a boundary separating state and private land. Set atop a high ridge, this line runs between Big Indian and Doubletop Mountains, and successful bushwhacks often include this benchmark. A path parallels this border. In places, this trail deteriorates, but the route remains visible.

Motor vehicles provide the quest's initial transportation, but their usefulness ends at the Seager parking area. The path's beginning stretch is a yellow-marked trail. It winds along Dry Brook's western bank, the playful water often turning the trail to mud. Small stands of mature hemlock shade the trail and surrounding mountainside. Other areas support a young forest of mixed species. Logging occurred into the mid-1900s in this area. Timber cutting and subsequent flooding removed the mature hardwoods once gracing these banks. Roaring chainsaws and raging floodwaters filled this area with activity. Now the gentle rustle of leaves and gurgle of water fill the air. The trail slowly heads upward, shifting with the valley and lifting through Shandaken Hollow (for an additional description of this area see the Big Indian section).

Once the trail begins to descend Big Indian's southern slopes, it encounters private land. Following this boundary along a south-southwest course, it will trace the ridgeline leading to Doubletop's upper elevations. This perimeter trail separates state and private land all the way to Doubletop. The trail gently falls from Big Indian's main ridge, makes a short ascent, and then crosses a small summit. Stunted hardwoods and balsam fir stands line this path.

Poorly drained, the flat ridgetop is often wet, soaking both vegetation and unprepared footwear. Some distinctive communities grow along this little used trail. One is a balsam fir stand underlain by lush grasses, mosses, and bog. With the fir's lower branches absent, the clear understory reveals a bright green floor of grass and a dark green needle ceiling. Quiet and serene, this spot is more akin to Maine than the Catskills.

To the north are Dry Brook's headwaters. A few peeks into the valley reveal a maturing northern hardwood forest. Like many areas in the Catskills, these healthy-appearing slopes retain many signs of past logging. Cut stumps, wider than most trees currently growing on those slopes, stud the ground. Old root scars attest to past encounters with mechanized logging equipment. The forest's largest trees show poor form and signs of weakness. Spared from these slopes' selective logging decades ago, their poor quality made harvest economically unviable. While the selective logging left some forest structure intact, these genetic inferiors repopulated the forest. In some ways the forest below is more of a tree recovery ward than anything approaching pristine wilderness.

The saddle between the small unnamed peak and Doubletop is another good orientation beacon. A series of red-painted trees follows the ridgeline denoting the state-land boundary. Rarely shown on maps, this thin trail of scuffed ground is often hard to follow. Only the blazed trees and accompanying signs provide orientation. From the 3,000-foot saddle the final assault on Doubletop begins.

As the border trail nears Doubletop it dissipates, but following the mountain's incline is easy. Spring decorates this area with hordes of spring beauties, trout lilies, and purple trillium. The climb continues into a spruce-fir forest. Thick hobblebush stands, covered with white flowers in May, mix with striped maple, mountain maple, yellow birch, paper birch, and mountain-ash. An increase in slope hides Doubletop's summits among the surrounding tree clutter.

Wreckage from a small plane crash ornaments Doubletop's eastern face. Chunks of warped, twisted, and disfigured aluminum mar the ground. Nature won this battle between man and the elements, but not without a price. The plane's fateful path through the forest shows to the observant eye. The plane's final resting place also marks the journey's steepest uphill climb. The trail often fades into the forest, and the unstable slopes make it hard to remain steady. Small cliffs adorn the mountain face, and rocks pull loose under gravity's influence. The ascent is brisk. Balsam fir, dwarfed American beech, and yellow birch compose the high elevation forest. Cool breezes rattle the trees, spreading the balsam's sweet smell.

Stunted trees provide an open vista to the east. Big Indian and Slide Mountains dominate the eastern sky. Fir and Spruce Mountains fill the land between them, with the Burroughs Range defining the eastern skyline. Eagle Mountain flanks Big Indian's northern slopes. Peekamoose, Table, and the smaller VanWyck lie to the southeast. Lone and Rocky Mountains trail northeast from Table. Panther Mountain rises beyond Eagle. Further north, Hunter, Westkill, and Plateau stand among the northern Catskill peaks. In the distance Overlook, Plattekill, and the Devil's Path sculpt the horizon.

Plane wreckage on the eastern slope of Doubletop.

The slope softens as the route approaches Doubletop's 3,840-foot southern summit, and a dense balsam fir forest covers the area. Here the state-land boundary line intersects the unmarked trail from Frost Valley. Along this southern route, two viewpoints overlook the Delaware basin.

As the land drops, a forest opening reveals a look north to Doubletop's true summit. The 3,680-foot peak dominates the immediate foreground. The dense balsam fir stand provides a distinct alpine character. Progress is difficult. A thin, intermittent path leads toward this pinnacle, but only a compass bearing and the search for higher terrain provide definitive guides. Once on Doubletop's northern summit, the trail reforms and heads toward the true summit.

Near the summit, a southwest-facing, exposed rock ledge breaks the monotony of fir trees. From this vantage, Balsam Lake Mountain and its fire tower lift in the west. Woodpecker Ridge descends south of Balsam Lake Mountain. Farther south, the Beaverkill Range wraps around many low hills and ridges.

Doubletop Mountain's true summit is beyond the viewpoint. The Catskill 3500 Club's orange sign-in box marks the spot. Many large fir trees and a thriving understory surround the area. Throughout this high elevation forest, dead fir trunks stretch decaying limbs to a sun they no longer need. A dense, dark green sea of needles blocks the sun and saturates the air with balsam. Doubletop's alpine forest is wondrous, but not hospitable. Dark humus, discarded needles, and scattered rock compose the land. A tangle of sharp, dead fir twigs often hide the ground. This place, free of human impact, is pleasant yet lonely. Completely free from civilization's sights and sounds, nature's randomness becomes overbearing. This unique place quickly becomes tiresome. The lowlands pull at the soul.

Part trail, part bushwhack, this challenging journey calls only to enthusiastic adventurers. With approaches from all four sides Doubletop, the western Catskills' deepest wilderness, provides many opportunities for exploration. Even after hiking Doubletop in the summer, the mountain offers another challenge as a winter hike.

BALSAM LAKE MOUNTAIN

Hike: Balsam Lake Mountain
Roundtrip Hiking Distance: 6.7 miles
County and Town: Ulster, Hardenburgh
Parking: Along Mill Brook Road (accessible via Dry Brook Road,
     Ulster County Route 49), 2.2 miles south of intersection
     with Ulster County Route 49.
Difficulty: moderate-difficult
Bushwhack: no
Elevation Gain: 1100 feet

Mile: 0.0: Begin Balsam Lake Mountain Trail (blue markers) at
     junction with Ulster County Route 49.
     2.2: Bear right at trail junction (red markers).
     3.1: Summit and fire tower.
     3.5: Lean-to.
     3.9: Trail ends at blue-marked trail. Turn left to return to
         starting point.
     4.5: Return to red trail's northern junction. Remain on blue
         trail.
     6.7: Return to starting point.

The westernmost Catskill peaks above 3,500 feet tail west from Slide Mountain. After leaping the Esopus Valley and topping Big Indian Mountain, the Catskills offer three more high peaks—Doubletop, Graham, and Balsam Lake Mountains. Farther west, and to the north and south, softer, rounded hills rise from ice-sculpted valleys. In contrast, the soaring peaks fill the eastern landscape.

Lifting 3,723 feet above sea level, Balsam Lake Mountain is among the Catskills' 20 highest peaks. The mountain's name derives from the

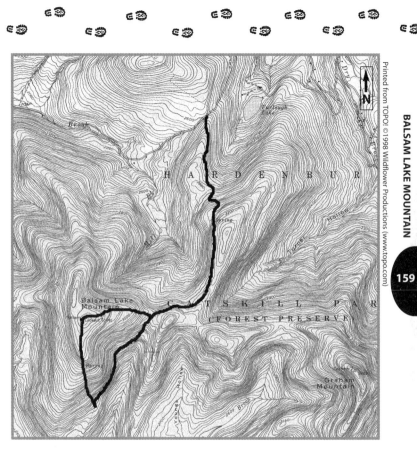

summit's dense balsam fir stands and the placid lake nestled into its southern flank. Balsam Lake Mountain's slopes provide many opportunities for scenic exploration. Spirited views introduce the surrounding terrain. The western perspective is a grand addition to the Catskills' viewsheds. Since it has a host of natural features and offers a pleasant hike to its summit, Balsam Lake Mountain receives more visitation than neighboring peaks

Budding from Ulster County Route 49, the trail begins with a moderate rise, but soon levels. Converted from an old road, the trail's origin remains apparent. After passing the summit spur trail, this old roadbed completes its five-mile trip to Balsam Lake. The same trip by car would require driving more than 20 miles. A reminder of the Catskills' past, this trail is from an era when development and tourism flourished. In that era, the timber-based economy stripped the land of its life force and much of its beauty. Today, as the land overcomes these past economic abuses, tourism returns to the reborn slopes.

A young forest dominates the trailside, confirmed by the small-diameter trees growing in even-aged stands. The vegetation weaves a green blanket over the logged slopes. Sunlight bathes the 50-foot-high forest canopy, but only reaches the understory in small patches and scattered flecks. The forest is a mix of sugar maple, American beech, and yellow birch. Ferns nettles, and jewelweed grow in the shaded understory. In late spring, jewelweed blooms highlight the path with orange and yellow, reflecting a mix of southern and northern sub-species.

Rock tripe, an edible, though unappealing lichen, colonizes many exposed sandstone outcrops. It is a thin, concave, brown organism that resembles a potato chip. When damp, it smells like a mushroom. Its mild flavor resembles Chinese mushrooms. Although not an appealing food, rock tripe will sustain a starving body.

Lichens are mutualistic associations of algae and fungus. The two lifeforms work together to survive in marginal habitats where neither could alone. They are often the first organisms to colonize an area. Rocks and tree bark provide typical lichen habitat. The algae make sugars via photosynthesis, and the fungus provides physical structure while collecting water and nutrients. Catskill lichens come in pink, gold, green, gray, and brown varieties.

In late summer, hosts of purple, yellow, and white asters decorate the forest floor, and the berry crop ripens. Forest cover thins as elevation increases, and the sunny patches hold many blackberry and raspberry plants. The plump purple and red berries, overpacked with juice, are a tasty trailside snack and a high-energy food for wildlife. Small and large animals alike love these annual treats. Birds dart in and out of the patch, grabbing a berry before heading for safety. Bears will sit and eat berries for hours, which in late summer can supply up to

70% of their diet. The berry season is a time of plenty in North America's eastern forests.

The trail winds up the ridgeline and moves into the wide notch separating Balsam Lake and Graham Mountains. Black cherry, easily identified by its charcoal-colored, potato chip bark, joins the forest. Wood sorrel, a small, edible plant, lines the trail. Oxalic acid gives the sorrel a lemony taste. In mid-spring its purple and white flowers complement the dark green, heart-shaped leaves. A naturalized European variety has a milder flavor and a yellow flower that blooms in late summer. It is common in open areas and along roadsides.

Looking east from Balsam Lake Mountain at Graham, Doubletop, Slide, Table, and Peekamoose.

Once above 3,000 feet, the forest community blends into an upper hardwood forest. Grass- and fern-filled meadows thrive beneath large canopy gaps. The additional sunlight warms and dries the environment. Hobblebush becomes the dominant understory species. Its rough leaves begin turning a deep maroon in late summer. The deep red leaves pose a striking contrast with the verdant forest. Many other of these sun-loving plants turn golden brown by mid-August.

Yellow birch trees are more common and larger than at lower elevations. Their twisted, spreading branches shade large areas. They are a hearty, cold-resistant species. Black cherry, a species associated with canopy gaps, is also common. Evergreen balsam fir begin to mix with the upper hardwoods. The gradation from northern hardwood to spruce-fir forest develops best on the north-facing slopes. Sheltered from the sun, these slopes have higher soil moisture, faster nutrient cycling, and cooler leaf surface temperatures.

After a long, steady climb through the ecotone, the trail forks with the larger trail continuing toward Balsam Lake. The western fork climbs Balsam Lake Mountain's summit. Once off the main road, the trail quickly gains elevation. Yellow birch and balsam fir co-dominate the forest, providing a patchwork of light and dark green. The trail loses its grading as it traces a series of sharp cliffs and gently sloping ledges. Exposed sandstone layers reveal the basis for these patterns. Blocky, but unfolded, these horizontal strata form the Catskills' distinctive stair-step topography. Unlike lower slopes where deep glacial tills cover large areas, the higher elevations received only a thin till layer. As a result, the area's bedrock shapes the surface.

Balsam Lake Mountain's highest elevations support few areas of solid forest. Peppered with blowdowns, dead trees, and bleached balsam fir trunks, the forest constantly changes. Cinnamon fern, hobblebush, and grasses bask in the sunlight. Changes in rock type accompany the change in vegetation. Catskill conglomerate, often called puddingstone, replaces the gray Hamilton sandstone. Small, round quartz pieces mark the white cement-like rock with red, gray, purple, and tan studs.

As the land rises, the northern and eastern skyline shows through the tree cover. Graham Mountain fills the foreground. The Panther

Mountain circle dominates the background. Sandwiched between these mountains is the Phoenicia-West Branch Trail. From south to north it crosses Eagle, Haynes, Balsam, and Belleayre Mountains. Some of Delaware County's highest points, including Dry Brook Ridge, Mount Pisgah and Plattekill Mountain, compose the northwestern terrain.

Balsam Lake Mountain's summit is an open field. Mature fir stands, fire cherry, and yellow birch surround the meadow. Blowdowns randomly slice the land. Hobblebush, the most common understory shrub, and mountain maple fill these sunny gaps. Dead trees and small swampy areas are common, a legacy of the glacially sculpted mountaintop. Soils are shallow and composed of rock, dark humus, and decaying fir needles. Large areas of exposed bedrock erupt from the wet ground. The poorly drained soil provides few nutrients and only minimal support. On the mountain's northern face, this high elevation swamp is a bog. Soft peat mats cover the ground. Sphagnum mosses and other acid-adapted plants create a distinctive flora.

Within the clearing's center rises one of the Catskills' few remaining towers. Aging guardians, the towers once helped protect the mountains from fire. Satellite imagery and air patrol now fulfill these duties. Efforts started in the late 1990s are working to restore the Catskills' remaining fire towers. On Balsam Lake Mountain, the restored tower is the only way to see beyond the thick stands of balsam fir trees covering the summit.

A 360-degree panorama opens from the fire sentry. Free of the ground's friction, the 3,000-foot jet stream roars to life. What were gentle breezes on the ground quickly become crisp, moving rivers of air. The flow batters and rattles the metal structure. One-sided flag trees confirm the westerly winds. Like the wind, the eye can race through the soft, peaceful landscapes. Balsam Lake Mountain provides a distinctive perspective. To the east are the Catskills' highest elevations with Slide and Table Mountains dominating the middle ground. Running between Slide and Balsam Lake Mountains are Graham and Doubletop Mountains. Northeast of these giants, above Dry Brook Valley, are Eagle, Haynes, Balsam, and Belleayre Mountains. Along the northeast horizon are the Devil's Path and the Blackheads. Hunter Mountain's 4,040-foot pinnacle verifies its claim as the Catskills' second-highest peak. Neighboring Balsam Lake Mountain to the northwest is Dry Brook Ridge, its summit marking the highest point in Delaware County. To the west and south, a series of hills roll into the Delaware and Susquehanna Valleys. The Shawangunks' long, knife-edged ridges slice through the southeastern view. Skytop, the stone tower above the Mohonk Mountain House, boldly rises from this ridgetop.

Paths descend to the north and south from the summit. Balsam Lake Mountain's southern slopes shelter a forest community different from its northern slopes. While balsam fir remains the dominant tree, the soil is darker—a deep, rich humus layer sits below a thick mat of decomposing needles. The ground is drier, and brittle grasses rustle in the breeze. Sun-exposed, open areas support fields of hay-scented fern. The sweet mix of hay and balsam are an olfactory treat. Against the backdrop of dark fir needles, the bright green fronds glow in the afternoon sun. Although dominant today, this forest community is only a slice in time. If the ground remains free of disturbance, trees will colonize the fern-covered slopes; if deprived of light, the ferns will die.

The trail briskly descends the mountain's southern face. The mountaintop shelters the land, harboring a lush northern hardwood forest of beech and birch. Wildflowers and berries abound. The path is only a thin dirt line, another contrast with the northern face's trail. Small streams caress and cross the pathway. The shaded slopes project a comfortable, hospitable atmosphere.

Periglacial boulders and rocks, most placed just after the retreat of the continental ice sheet, lay scattered about Balsam Lake Mountain's southern face. Cracked, broken, and released through constant freezing, thawing, and gravity, these rock rivers tumbled down the mountainside. Once the Wisconsin Ice Sheet retreated from New York, the warmer conditions slowed this process. Lichens and mosses now colonize the exposed surfaces, and pockets of organic soil develop between the rocks. In a few of the deeper pockets, a few small trees survive.

The fast descent brings the trail into taller, more protected forests. The thin path ends when it merges with the old road connecting Balsam Mountain Lake (and the headwaters of the Beaverkill) and Ulster County Route 49. Once heading north, the road follows a steeply graded slope. The sharp slopes of Balsam Lake Mountain lift directly west, while a shadowy downslope leads into Black Brook below. Soon, the trail returns to the notch between Graham and Balsam Lake Mountains where a classic northern hardwood mix of yellow birch, American beech, and sugar maple covers the slopes. Although this are is still recovering from past logging, sheltered areas can support taller trees. Besides providing greater shelter than the mountain's higher elevations, the gap has a longer growing season, and deeper, more fertile soils. The dense leaf canopy retains moisture, allowing mosses to thrive. Once the old road intersects the trail climbing Balsam Lake Mountain's northern face, the return trip follows the original path.

Balsam Lake Mountain has unique perspectives of Catskill topography, geography, and ecology. Nature's stories spin different tales here. Balsam Lake Mountain has persevered through the ages and continues to make an aggressive stand in the hostile conditions. Capped with a lush cover of dark fir, the summit displays many subalpine characteristics. Balsam Lake Mountain is among the Catskills' gems, and to skip this destination is to miss one of its brightest facets.

DRY BROOK RIDGE

Hike: Dry Brook Ridge
Roundtrip Hiking Distance: 7.0 miles
County and Town: Ulster and Delaware, Hardenburgh and
Middletown
Parking: At the end of Soderlind Road, just south of Arkville via
Dry Brook Road.
Difficulty: moderate-difficult
Bushwhack: no
Elevation Gain: 2000 feet

Mile: 0.0: Begin German Hollow Trail (yellow markers) at end of
Soderlind Road.
0.7: Lean-to.
1.5: Trail ends at Dry Brook Ridge Trail (blue markers). Turn
south.
3.5: Reach second set of views. Summit slightly east of trail.
Return via same route.
7.0: Return to Soderlind Road.

Dry Brook Ridge lies along the Catskill high peaks' western fringe. At 3,460 feet it is Delaware County's highest point. The Ulster-Delaware County border slices the mountain's main ridge. West of Dry Brook Ridge, the topography becomes gentler and few places top 3,000 feet. With only westward opening views, Dry Brook Ridge shuns its higher, eastern neighbors. Neither the trail nor the mountain's ledges permit an eastern vista. From its overlooks, Dry Brook Ridge appears the highest point around. Perhaps this deception is purposeful, allowing Dry Brook Ridge to boast of being the highest mountain visible. The

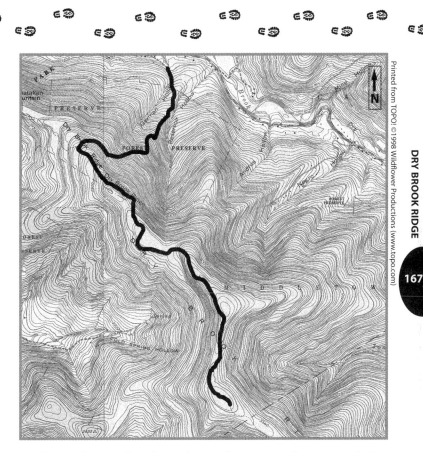

evidence refutes such a charge, but with its extraordinary west-facing views one can ignore or even sympathize with Dry Brook Ridge's motives.

Three main trails provide access to Dry Brook Ridge. German Hollow is the shortest route, a seven-mile round trip. The steep trail quickly completes most of the climb, rising from 1,500 feet to 2,800 feet during the first mile and a half. Once on Dry Brook Ridge's main ridge, steep slopes mix with level areas, providing welcome rest to the adventurer. Then the mountain provides another steep climb, and the trail reaches Dry Brook Ridge's open sandstone ledges. From these ledges a peaceful afternoon passes in the wink of an eye, but can remain in memory forever.

Late spring makes for great hiking. New leaves cover only the lower elevations, permitting unobstructed views from the mountaintops. The neighboring valleys wear cheery shades of spring green. Flower-lined trails brighten the mountain slopes, and the staggered blooming schedules make the trip a journey through time. Flowers opening almost a month earlier at the mountains' bases now highlight ridgetops. Without spring leaves, a mountaintop of sticks, branches, and trunks contrasts with lush bottomland forests. Late spring also means courtship and child rearing among the animal kingdom. Animal calls, from chipmunks to ruffed grouse, echo through the forest.

The German Hollow Trail starts as a walk into darkness. Heavy shade contrasts with the sunny parking area. Cool air bathes the path as it climbs into a shadowy hemlock forest. Young beech and yellow birch leaves accent the hemlocks' dark needles. Old logging trails form the sunken trail, and the deeply eroded path cuts a scar through the land. The forest seems to reject this inhospitable path, and high, banked walls separate it from the healthy second growth.

Few trees are wider than a foot in diameter. In another two centuries this forest will attain maturity. The area's youth shows among the bright clearings. Grasses and scattered shrubs bask in the sunlight. Flecks of golden sunshine dance on meadow plants. Violets, from purple to white to blue, line the trail as it tours the open spaces. Stone walls, markers of farmers' fields a century ago, crisscross the area. Despite a half century of neglect, the rock walls remain staunchly entrenched, drawing vestigial lines about the ecosystem.

As the trail passes a lean-to and makes a sharp switchback, it begins a transition. No longer will meadows mix with the forest. The trail leaves German Hollow's shelter and starts a steady, often steep, climb to Dry Brook Ridge's summit. The forest is a collection of beech, yellow birch, and sugar maple, along with an occasional northern red oak and white ash. Striped maple and beech saplings dominate the understory, their bright leaves complementing spring's flowers. A verdant blanket of ferns and herbaceous plants cover the ground. Streams of running water and frozen rock flow across the trail and down the mountainside. With thicker soils than those of the eastern Catskills, the forest grows fuller.

A large chipmunk population lives among the roots, shrubs, downed logs, and rocks. They dart about the forest searching for food, while ever wary of danger. Chipmunk populations explode when winters are mild and food plentiful. Easy winters allow a survival rate three times greater than average. Local populations expand until food sources run out, unleashing starvation and disease.

Chipmunk calls of danger are quick, sharp, bird-like chirps. A sprint to a nearby hiding place usually follows the alert. Often, the danger signal will accompany the run to safety, or comes a moment before the small, furry blur disappears into a rock crevice or beneath a fallen log. The warning alerts other nearby chipmunks to danger, but reveals the caller's presence. They remain hidden until hunger or curiosity force their never-ending search for food to continue. Despite

Looking east from Balsam Lake Mountain at Graham, Doubletop, Slide, Table, and Peekamoose.

the chipmunks' warning system, they fall prey to owls, hawks, foxes, and snakes. It is their ability to reproduce that insures the chipmunk's survival.

Steep slopes quickly lead the trail higher. The terrain is a battle with gravity, rock rivers, boulders, soil, and logs. Spring retreats as elevation increases, and the leafless trees allow direct sunlight to warm the ground. Spring beauties and trout lilies announce spring's arrival. The trail's slope moderates as it approaches the main ridge. Glacially carved sandstone ledges form the rounded contours. The path then reaches Dry Brook's main ridge and joins the Margaretville Trail.

Forest character changes atop the main ridge. The higher elevations bring stronger winds, colder temperatures, and thinner soils. Treetops drop to 30 feet. Sugar maple almost disappear, while oak and ash completely exit the forest. Yellow birch becomes the dominant tree, its stilted roots wrapping about rocks and logs. Beech also remain common, along with hobblebush, striped maple, and mountain maple. New forest members include black cherry and mountain-ash. Many of the cherry trees grow straight and tall, desirable for commercial harvest; however, the people's will, expressed through the State Constitution, preserves these forests for future generations.

As the summit lifts along the main ridge, outcrops of ice-carved bedrock appear alongside the trail. The outcrops create a stair step topography typical of the Catskills' higher elevations. Mostly free of glacial till, the poorly drained ledges form small marshes, bogs, and pools. Exposed bedrock cliffs support lichens, grasses, and a few struggling trees.

After traversing the long northeast-trending ridge, the stair steps lead to Dry Brook Ridge's northern summit. Birds, small mammals, and insects abound in the stunted hardwood forest. Hobblebush and small cherries fill the understory. The sandstones composing Dry Brook Ridge's summit are less blocky and erosion-resistant than in the eastern Catskills. They are darker and show strong cross-bedding.

Dry Brook Ridge offers two sets of western vistas. The sets are similar, but the first is more impressive—it sits along a 150-foot sandstone ledge and reveals a 180-degree panorama. Tranquil greens, blues, and browns mix well with a warm afternoon nap.

Dry Brook Ridge's true peak rises south of this ledge. As the trail continues south, it leads to Mill Brook Ridge. Forming the southern horizon, this glacially scoured ridgeline is the westernmost Catskill Mountain. Mill Brook Ridge grades westward toward Cross Mountain, the western Catskills' first hill. Few of these hills reach 3,000 feet. Plattekill Mountain is the exception, its sharp form poking to 3,375 feet.

Dry Brook Ridge's western slopes drain into Huckleberry Hollow. The glacially rounded valley leads to the Pepacton Reservoir, its blue water contrasting with the greening valleys. Part of New York City's water supply, this reservoir dams the Delaware River's East Branch.

The trail continues to Dry Brook Ridge's triangular summit. Unlike its eastern neighbors, no spruce-fir forest grows on the 3,460-foot peak. Without this dark crown, Dry Brook Ridge is a monochrome monument. South of the summit, the path crosses into Ulster County and heads for Balsam Lake Mountain. A return trip through German Hollow, however, is the shortest route to civilization. Spring accelerates along the descending route, adding a month of foliage in only a couple of hours. Leaves sprout, the air warms, flowers bloom and become fruit. Dry Brook Ridge well represents the western Catskills, revealing outstanding vistas, diverse wildlife, and provides a challenging day hike.

Appendix A: CATSKILL ELEVATIONS

Rank	Mountain	Elevation (feet)
1	Slide	4,180
2	Hunter	4,040
3	Black Dome	3,990
4	Blackhead	3,940
5	Thomas Cole	3,940
6	Westkill	3,880
7	Graham	3,868
8	Doubletop	3,860
9	Cornell	3,860
10	Table	3,847
11	Peekamoose	3,843
12	Plateau	3,840
13	Sugarloaf	3,800
14	Wittenberg	3,780
15	Southwest Hunter	3,740
16	Lone	3,721
17	Balsam Lake	3,720
18	Panther	3,720
19	Big Indian	3,700
20	Friday	3,694
21	Rusk	3,680
22	Kaaterskill High Peak	3,655
23	Twin	3,680
24	Balsam Cap	3,623
25	Fir	3,620
26	Northdome	3,610
27	Balsam	3,600
28	Bearpen	3,600
29	Eagle	3,600
30	Indian Head	3,573
31	Sherill	3,540

32	Vly	3,529
33	Windham High Peak	3,524
34	Halcott	3,520
35	Rocky	3,508
36	Mill Brook Ridge	3,480
37	Dry Brook Ridge	3,460
38	Woodpecker Ridge	3,460
39	Olderbark	3,440
40	Roundtop (by KHP)	3,440
41	Roundtop (by Bearpen)	3,440
42	Huntersfield	3,423
43	Belleayre	3,420

Other Selected Elevations

Place	Elevation
Moresville Range	3,220
Onteora	3,220
Utsayantha	3,214
Giant Ledge	3,200
Burnt Knob	3,180
Overlook	3,150
East Jewett Range	3,140
Plattekill	3,100
High Point	3,098
Tremper	2,740

Appendix B: ROUTES DESCRIBED TO PEAKS WITH TRAILS

The Ashokan Reservoir: (driving tour along Basin Road, Route 28A, Monument Road, and Reservoir Road)

Mount Tremper:

Mile: 0.0: Trail begins along Old Route 28, just southeast of Phoenicia (red markers).

        2.9: Summit of Tremper; return via same route.

        5.8: Return to trailhead.

Overlook:

Mile: 0.0: Leave parking area in saddle between Overlook and Guardian Mountains.

        1.1: Dirt road splits, take northern (left) fork.

        1.8: Reach ruins of Overlook Mountain House.

        1.9: Leave dirt road, heading south for escarpment trail.

        2.6: Reach open ledges; turn back along dirt road.

        2.7: Pass fire tower; continue back to parking area.

        5.2: Return to parking area.

Ashokan High Point:

Mile: 0.0: Trail begins along Peekamoose Road. Trail crosses Kanape Brook.

        1.6: Pass flat, open meadow.

        2.7: Reach notch between Ashokan High Point and Mombaccus Mountain. Turn north (left).

        3.6: Summit of Ashokan High Point. Excellent viewpoint located .3 miles to east-southeast (bushwhack).

        3.8: Path continues west to various viewpoints. Return via same route.

        4.9: Return to notch between Ashokan High Point and Mombaccus.

        6.0: Pass meadow.

        7.6: Return to parking area.

Slide Mountain:

Mile: 0.0: Trail begins at parking area along County Route 47 after Winnisook Lake (yellow markers).

0.6: Trail merges with old road.

0.8: Turn east (left) onto Wittenberg-Cornell-Slide Trail (red markers).

2.2: Pass Curtis Ormsbee Trail on right. Views lie a small distance down the trail.

2.8: Summit of Slide; return via same route.

4.8: Return to yellow-marked trail. Turn north (right).

5.6: Return to parking area.

Giant Ledge:

Mile: 0.0: Trail begins at parking area along County Route 47 at sharp turn (yellow markers).

0.7: Reach notch between Giant Ledge and Slide. Turn north (left, blue markers).

1.5: Summit of Giant Ledge, views from eastern and western faces. Return via same route.

2.3: Return to notch, turn west (right).

3.0: Return to parking area.

Panther Mountain: (need 2 vehicles to complete trip via Fox Hollow)

Mile: 0.0: Trail begins at parking area along County Route 47 at sharp turn (yellow markers) and follows route to Giant Ledge.

1.5: Summit of Giant Ledge.

2.0: Notch between Giant Ledge and Panther.

3.3: Summit of Panther. Begin descent into Fox Hollow (can return by same route or Fox Hollow).

6.9: Pass Fox Hollow lean-to.

7.5: Reach Fox Hollow parking area.

Lone, Rocky, Balsam Cap, and Dink Mountains: (all trail-less)

Cornell and Wittenberg:

Mile: 0.0: Trail begins by Woodland Valley Campground and parking area.

   2.6: Pass spur trail to Terrace Mountain.

   3.9: Summit of Wittenberg.

   4.2: Reach notch between Wittenberg and Cornell.

   4.7: Short spur trail leads east (left) to Cornell's summit. Trail begins to descend.

   4.8: Two excellent views. Retrace route to return.

   5.7: Pass summit of Wittenberg.

   9.6: Return to Woodland Valley and parking area.

Belleayre Mountain:

Mile: 0.0: Begin by following railroad track west off Pine Hill's Mill Street.

   0.5: Turn south onto Cathedral Glen Trail (blue markers).

   1.2: Meet up with ski trail.

   1.6: Leave ski trail, head east.

   1.8: Junction with Belleayre Ridge Trail (red markers). Turn west.

   2.5: Reach top of ski area. Return east on Belleayre Ridge Trail.

   3.5: Belleayre's summit. Turn north on Pine Hill-West Branch Trail (blue markers).

   6.3: Return to Pine Hill; follow old railroad bed west to parking area.

Balsam Mountain:

Mile: 0.0: Trail starts along Rider Hollow Road (red markers).

   0.3: Pass lean-to.

   1.6: Reach notch and junction with Pine Hill-West Branch Trail (blue markers). Turn north.

   2.3: Summit of Balsam Mountain.

   3.6: Junction with Mine Hollow Trail (yellow markers). Turn west.

   4.6: Rejoin Oliveria-Mapledale Trail. Turn west.

   5.0: Return to Rider Hollow Road.

Haynes and Eagle Mountains:

Mile:
- 0.0: Trail starts along Rider Hollow Road (red markers).
- 0.3: Pass lean-to.
- 1.6: Reach notch and junction with Pine Hill-West Branch Trail (blue markers). Turn south.
- 2.5: Summit of Haynes Mountain. Continue south.
- 4.0: Summit of Eagle Mountain.
- 5.3: Junction with Seager-Big Indian Trail. Return via route taken.
- 10.6 Return to Rider Hollow Road.

Big Indian Mountain:

Mile:
- 0.0: Begin Seager-Big Indian Mountain Trail (yellow markers) off Dry Brook Road.
- 1.3: Cross Dry Brook Stream, enter Shandaken Hollow.
- 2.1: Pass Shandaken Brook lean-to.
- 3.0: Trail ends at Pine Hill-West Branch Trail (blue markers). Turn south.
- 4.8: Trail's crest on Big Indian. Bushwhack east to summit.
- 5.0: Reach Big Indian's summit. Return via same route.
- 10.0: Return to Seager-Big Indian Mountain trailhead.

Peekamoose and Table: (one-way hike, requires two vehicles)

Mile:
- 0.0: Parking area at terminus of Denning Road (yellow markers).
- 1.1: Junction with Peekamoose-Table Trail. Turn east (right, blue markers).
- 1.4: Denning lean-to.
- 3.9: Summit of Table.
- 4.6: Notch between Table and Cornell.
- 4.9: Summit of Peekamoose. Begin descent.
- 5.6: Pass old trail on left.
- 8.2: Reach parking area along Peekamoose Road.

Doubletop Mountain:

Mile: 0.0: Begin Seager-Big Indian Mountain Trail (yellow markers) off Dry Brook Road.

1.3: Cross Dry Brook Stream, enter Shandaken Hollow.

2.1: Pass Shandaken Brook lean-to.

3.0: Trail ends at Pine Hill-West Branch Trail (blue markers). Turn south.

4.8: Trail's crest on Big Indian.

5.0: Encounter boundary of state land (poorly marked).

5.8: Cross lowpoint between Big Indian and Doubletop Mountains.

6.4: Doubletop's northern summit.

6.6: Doubletop's southern (true) summit. Trace the route back to Seager Parking Area.

13.2: Return to Seager parking area.

Balsam Lake Mountain:

Mile: 0.0: Begin Balsam Lake Mountain Trail (blue markers) at junction with Ulster County Route 49.

2.2: Bear right at trail junction (red markers).

3.1: Summit and fire tower.

3.5: Lean-to.

3.9: Trail ends at blue-marked trail. Turn left to return to starting point.

4.5: Return to red trail's northern junction. Remain on blue trail.

6.7: Return to starting point.

Dry Brook Ridge:

Mile: 0.0: Begin German Hollow Trail (yellow markers) at end of Soderlind Road.

0.7: Lean-to.

1.5: Trail ends at Dry Brook Ridge Trail (blue markers). Turn south.

3.5: Reach second set of views. Summit slightly east of trail. Return via same route.

7.0: Return to Soderlind Road

ABOUT THE AUTHOR

Ed Henry grew up in the Catskill Mountains, just outside of Woodstock. He has been exploring and writing about the Appalachian Mountains and surrounding regions for the past twenty years, first as a boy scout, then as a writer and photographer. The Shawangunks' long, rugged ridge has been a familiar part of Ed's life. From the sharp form of Snake Hill all the way south to High Point in New Jersey, Ed has hiked and photographed this unique ridge.

Besides his adventures in the Gunks and the Catskills, Ed has worked as a park ranger in the Shenandoah and Great Smoky Mountains National Parks. He also has worked for the U.S. Forest Service, and currently works for the U.S. Fish and Wildlife Service and the 540-unit National Wildlife Refuge System. One of these refuges, Shawangunk Grasslands NWR, is included in this book.

Ed Henry is the author of two books on the Catskill Mountains, Books One & Two of *Catskill Trails: A Ranger's Guide to the High Peaks* (Black Dome Press), plus numerous magazine articles. He has a master's degree in forest ecology from SUNY's College of Environmental Science and Forestry in Syracuse, New York.

Ed lives with his family in western Massachusetts, but frequently returns to his favorite trails in the Gunks and Catskills.

✓ YES, I'd like to order:

Book One of *Catskill Trails: The Northern Catskills.*
Enclosed is my check, or credit card payment information.

No. of copies	Price	Total
	@ $14.95	
	Plus shipping ($2.50 for 1st book $.50 each additional)	
	NYS residents add 8% sales tax	
	TOTAL	

Name _____

Address _____

City _____

State _____ Zip _____

Telephone _____

<u>Credit Card Customers</u>

Signature _____

Visa or MC # _____

Exp. Date _____

Telephone # _____

<u>Mail this coupon with check enclosed to:</u>
Black Dome Press, 1011 Route 296, Hensonville, NY 12439.
Credit card customers may mail or fax to 518-734-5802
or call to order 800-513-9013

ALSO AVAILABLE FROM BLACK DOME PRESS

For ordering information or a complete catalog: Black Dome Press, 1011 Route 296, Hensonville, NY, 12439. Tel: 800-513-9013 (orders only, please) or 518-734-6357 (editorial). Website: www.blackdomepress.com

CATSKILL TRAILS: A RANGER'S GUIDE TO THE HIGH PEAKS
Book One: the Northern Catskills
by Edward G. Henry
The first Book of Catskill Trails includes hikes through some of the most magnificent scenery in the Eastern United States-the high peaks and wilderness of the northern tier of the Catskill State Park and Preserve-taking you to the highest waterfall in New York State, incredible vistas of the Hudson Valley and western New England, and the Catskills' famous "cloves"-steep, rocky mountain valleys that define "picturesque" but defy access to all but the hardiest hikers. Hikes include the awe-inspiring four-state views of the Eastern Escarpment trails, the Blackhead and Devil's Path Ranges, Roundtop, Kaaterskill High Peak, Bearpen, Huckleberry Point, and many more!
5 x 7, 184 pages, photos, maps, key to hikes, paper, $14.95

THE HOUSE IN THE WOODS
by Arthur Henry, Foreword and Afterword by Donald Oakes, Introduction by Alf Evers, Preface by Neda M. Westlake
Young urban professionals realize a dream of escaping to a mountaintop, building their own house and subsisting off the land. A contemporary tale? Hardly. This book spans the years 1899-1903. The setting is the wild and remote Catskill Mountain region known today as Platte Clove. The author is a close literary friend of Theodore Dreiser. At once a fascinating window on manners and mores in rural America a century ago, an important work for Dreiser scholars, a charming, beautifully written memoir of the age-old quest for "the simple life," and a poignant lesson on how reality can fall tragically short of dreams.
6 x 9, 232 pages, paper, photos, $15.95

O. & W. The Long Life and Slow Death of the New York, Ontario & Western Railway
By William F. Helmer
Over 100 photographs and illustrations grace this history of the Ontario & Western-the O&W, or, as both boosters and detractors referred to it in its later years, the "Old & Weary." The O&W line operated from 1869-1957, and ran from Oswego on Lake Ontario to New York City, passing through the "midlands" and southern counties of New York State, with spurs to Utica, Kingston, Port Jervis, and Scranton, PA. Filled with colorful characters and miscellaneous machinery, O. & W. chronicles almost a century of alternating hope and heartache, prosperity and poverty, dignity and degradation, and the passing of part of a way of life now gone from the American scene.
6 x 9, 232 pages, maps, photos, illustrations, $15.95

THE HUDSON: From the Wilderness to the Sea
by Benson Lossing, Introduction by Pete Seeger.
Eye-witness impressions written a century and a half ago. The author, with sketchbook always in hand, traveled by horse and carriage along the banks of the Hudson River from New York City to the Adirondacks, staying in local inns and looking up local storytellers and historians. Lossing unforgettably captured pre-Civil War America, when NYC numbered 300,000 people, steamboats and railroads had just begun plying the Hudson River and its banks, and every inch of the Hudson River Valley was pastureland and farmland surrounding a few sleepy villages and a handful of bustling river ports. Over 300 wood engravings.
6 x 9, 472 pages, illustrations, paper, $19.95

RIP VAN WINKLE RAILROADS by William F. Helmer
Filled with over 100 illustrations, including many rare archival photographs from private collections, this is the history of the narrow gauge railroads—the Canajoharie & Catskill Railroad, the Catskill Mountain Railway, the Catskill & Tannersville Railway, and the Otis Elevating Railway—which steamed through the northeastern Catskill Mountains during the 19th-century heyday of the grand hotels.
8 x 11, 150 pages, photos, illus., maps, index, paper, $21.95

PIONEER DAYS IN THE CATSKILL HIGH PEAKS Tannersville & the Region Around
by Leah Showers Wiltse, edited by Shirley Wiltse Dunn
Shortly after the Revolutionary War, the first pioneers followed old Indian trails up the mountains to carve out homesteads in the High Peak region of the Catskills, in what is now Tannersville, Haines Falls, East Jewett and Onteora Park. In the true voice of the mountains, this oral history, passed down through generations of the author's family, tells the story of how the High Peak Wilderness was tamed.
6 x 9, 160 pages, 80 photos, illus., index, paper, $15.95

VIDEOFREEX America's First Pirate TV Station & the Catskills Collective that Turned it on
by Parry D. Teasdale
A saga of the freewheeling '60s, complete with Hells Angels, Abbie Hoffman, the Black Panther Party, and FBI surveillance. This is the insider's tale of the high-tech hijinks and groundbreaking innovations of a hippie collective near Woodstock, New York, which operated an experimental—and highly illegal—unlicensed TV broadcasting station, and in the process pioneered TV techniques which have become commonplace today
6 x 9, 200 pages, photos, illus., index, paper, $16.95

SARATOGA LOST: Images of Victorian America, by Robert Joki
The Golden Age of the "Queen of Spas" (1860-1890s), when the rich and famous came every summer to "take the waters". Over 300 Victorian-era photographs grace this elegant volume comprising the first comprehensive pictorial of 19th-century Saratoga Springs. *Robert Joki helps preserve an important chapter in the history of 19th-century Saratoga Springs.*—from the foreword by Marylou Whitney.
8 1/2 x 11, 208 pp, paper, photos, index, illustrations, $24.95

JOHN BURROUGHS An American Naturalist, by Edward J. Renehan, Jr.
The first full biography of the dean of American nature writers to be published since 1925. [Renehan reveals] *a far more complex and interesting man than other biographers have described. ... In this thoughtful biography we are shown the once sainted 'Sage of Slabsides' as a flesh-and-blood traveler in a now-vanished world.*—New York Times Sunday Book Review
6 x 9, 400 pp, paper, photos, index, $19.95

MY TIMES IN THE HUDSON VALLEY The Insider's Guide to Historic Homes, Scenic Drives, Restaurants, Museums, Farm Produce & Points of Interest
by Harold Faber, former Hudson Valley correspondent for *The New York Times*
This is a guide unlike any other—from Lake Tear of the Clouds in the Adirondacks to NYC's bustling Harbor, a region as rich and varied as any to be found.
6 x 9, 260 pp, maps, illustrations, paper, $16.95

CHRONICLES OF THE HUDSON Three Centuries of Travel & Adventure
by Roland Van Zandt, Introduction by John Cronin, Riverkeeper
Captures 300 years of travelers' tales of adventure on America's own Hudson River from its Adirondack headwaters at Lake Tear of the Clouds to New York City's bustling harbor. In coming to chart the River's path, the men and women chronicled here became participants in its illustrious history, including explorers and travelers from Robert Juet, navigator aboard Henry Hudson's pioneering Half Moon, to General Lafayette and Henry James. *Reminds us forcibly of how much of the Hudson we have lost, and how urgent it is that we preserve the ... beauty that remains along its banks.*—The New York Times
9 x 10, 384 pp, paper, 51 Illustrations & maps, index, $25.95

THE LIFE AND WORKS OF THOMAS COLE
by Louis Legrand Noble, edited by Elliot S. Vesell
Artists flocked to New York's Catskill Mountains and Hudson Valley to confront the wilderness and emulate Cole's vision, and America's first indigenous art movement was born—the Hudson River School of landscape painting. This is the primary source of biographical material about Cole, constructed from his own writings—his poetry, essays and descriptions—woven together with narrative and commentary by a man who knew him well.
6 x 9, 400 pages, 25 plates, paper, $21.95

DIAMOND STREET The Story of the Little Town with the Big Red Light District
by Bruce Edward Hall
Hudson, NY, pop. 8000, a Norman Rockwell painting in motion, with one big difference—for almost two centuries this little city by the Hudson River held an international reputation as a center for corruption and vice.
6 x 9, 222 pp, 43 illustrations, Paper, $13.95

THE CATSKILL MOUNTAIN HOUSE America's Grandest Hotel by Roland Van Zandt
Captures the birth, glory and fiery death of America's premier mountain resort. Best known for inspiring the Hudson River School of painting, for 140 years the Catskill

Mountain House stood on a rock shelf above the Hudson Valley and facing the River.
6 x 9, 416 pp, 94 illustrations, 9 maps, Paper: $21.95

PORTRAITS OF PRIDE The Mountaintop Remembers by Richard Winter
As family farms fade away, taking with them a way of life and a lifelong sense of values instilled in earliest childhood, the last remaining old-timers take a look at the present day and compare it with the world they knew.
8 x 10, 208 pp, 61 photographs, Paper, $19.95

THE GREENE COUNTY CATSKILLS A History
by Field Horne, Introduction by Mario Cuomo
Four hundred years of Hudson Valley history! *Historian Field Horne...is a font of knowledge and lively chronicler of folklore. The enchanting full-color cover—with Rip asleep on an old postcard of famous Catskill sites—is worth the price of the book.*—Albany Times Union
8 x 11, 236 pp, 121 illustrations, Cloth: $35.95
Greene County Bicentennial trade paper edition: $25.95

THE HUCKLEBERRY PICKERS A Raucous History of the Shawangunk Mountains
by Marc B. Fried
The hard-working days and rowdy nights of the squatters' camps, summer home to the berry-pickers—an isolated, clannish, proud and independent community of free spirits and families struggling to survive—generations of whom converged on the winding trails and rocky overlooks of the Minnewaska and Ellenville parklands to harvest the "blue gold" of the Shawangunks.
6 x 9, 164 pp, maps & illustrations, Paper, $14.95

KAATERSKILL From the Catskill Mountain House to the Hudson River School
by The Mountain Top Historical Society
The home and haunt of America's Romantic-era landscape painters, the grand hotels, and the golden age of railroads. *For those interested in the Catskills, or in mountains, or in history, or in fascinating places.*— Adirondack Mountain Club
5 x 8, 120 pp, 33 illustrations, Paper, $13.95

THE OLD EAGLE-NESTER The Lost Legends of the Catskills by Doris West Brooks
This is wonderful stuff, some of it funny, some of it frightening, all of it entertaining.— Dutchess Magazine
6 x 9, 128 pp, original illustrations, Paper, $13.95

A WAR TO PETRIFY THE HEART, The Civil War Letters of a Dutchess County, NY Volunteer
by Richard T. Van Wyck. Edited, with notes and chapter introductions.
This is one of the great eye-witness accounts of history in-the-making. *You can pretty much dip anywhere among Van Wyck's writings and come up with pay dirt.*—The Civil War Courier. Comprised of 197 letters, plus field journal entries.
6 x 9, 400 pages, 60 illustrations, Paper: $14.95, Cloth: $35.95